Creation as an Introduction
to Christian Thought

Creation as an Introduction to Christian Thought

HENRY VANDER GOOT

WIPF & STOCK · Eugene, Oregon

CREATION AS AN INTRODUCTION TO CHRISTIAN THOUGHT

Copyright © 2025 Henry Vander Goot. All rights reserved. Except for brief quotations in critical publications or reviews, no part of this book may be reproduced in any manner without prior written permission from the publisher. Write: Permissions, Wipf and Stock Publishers, 199 W. 8th Ave., Suite 3, Eugene, OR 97401.

Wipf & Stock
An Imprint of Wipf and Stock Publishers
199 W. 8th Ave., Suite 3
Eugene, OR 97401

www.wipfandstock.com

PAPERBACK ISBN: 979-8-3852-5231-2
HARDCOVER ISBN: 979-8-3852-5232-9
EBOOK ISBN: 979-8-3852-5233-6

VERSION NUMBER 07/29/25

Scripture quotes are from THE HOLY BIBLE, NEW INTERNATIONAL VERSION®, NIV® Copyright © 1973, 1978, 1984, 2011 by Biblica, Inc.® Used by permission. All rights reserved worldwide.

For Sipkje Walinga-Vander Goot, the first maternal light of my life, until taken from us in an untimely death in 1972; and for Mary Elizabeth Petter-Vander Goot, the current and primary light of my life until death do us part.

Contents

Preface | vii

CHAPTER 1
Introduction and a Statement of the Problem | 1

CHAPTER 2
Creation and the Necessity of Christian Philosophy | 23

CHAPTER 3
Mystery, the Limits of Knowledge, and Our Approach to Scripture | 33

CHAPTER 4
The Projection of Moses from out of His Own Completed World | 45

CHAPTER 5
What We Learn from Genesis 1 and 2 | 53

CHAPTER 6
Creation as Separation | 58

CHAPTER 7
Time as Seven Days/Seven Topics | 73

CHAPTER 8
Separate Structures and Biblical Directives | 78

CHAPTER 9
Sin and the Fall | 88

CHAPTER 10
The Eclipse of Creation | 96

Conclusion: Creation as the Foundation of Christian Thought | 132

Bibliography | 135

Index | 139

Preface

IN THE HISTORY OF THE ACADEMY there is a tradition of "the last lecture." It was a retiring professor's opportunity to summarize important themes in his thinking and hand out accolades to those who helped him pry open ideas that shaped his fascination over the years of his intellectual career. Once long ago I dreamed of being such a professor and actually started out along that path, eventually landing the position of a full professor with tenure. In my case there was another immigrant dream that tugged at me from the world of business. And so it was that after three decades immersed in books and ideas (as a student at various Christian institutions and then as a professor), I packed up my desk on campus and went into business. I formed a partnership with my college friend John Hultink (also a former immigrant), who had guts and energy and a razor-sharp mind for business. He continued on as a very successful entrepreneur, and I became the CEO of Bargain Books.

In the thirty-two years during which I ran a business, I did not forget where I started, and the ideas that first inspired me continued to inspire me. As launching into retirement, not from the academy but from the very practical world of commerce, a last statement seems more important to me than ever. A world-and life-view, first formed while a student and later developed as a professor, continued to shape my thinking. Those persons who helped me discover that worldview continued to be influences as I returned again and again to the foundational beliefs they helped me shape.

My worldview began to form during four college years at Calvin University (then Calvin College), where I majored in classics and philosophy and where H. Evan Runner was my professor of philosophy. At Calvin University my dear friend, teacher, and colleague Gordon Spykman helped me carry much of that influence forward by paving the way for me to join

Preface

the faculty of Calvin University, where I served as a professor for seventeen years.

There was another influence that stayed with me and continues to be part of my thinking. After graduating from college, I attended Princeton Seminary for three years, during which I earned a divinity degree. There I met my gracious senior thesis advisor, James Hastings Nichols, who was always willing to hear my thoughts about a Christian philosophy of creation, even though the intellectual atmosphere of the seminary was overwhelmingly under the influence of Karl Barth's "Christomonistic Unitarianism," as my gentlemanly professor of theology, George Hendry, often called it. In addition, my acquaintance with Professor Karlfried Froehlich, first formed at Princeton Seminary, led to a long and cordial friendship. Some years later during a year spent at the University of Tubingen, he graciously made his home near the university available to me, my wife, and our young daughter.

My transition from seminary to a graduate MA-PhD program in religion and theology at St. Michael's College of the University of Toronto was special beyond expectations. There I was able to develop a deep and abiding respect for the Catholic Church, open as it was in its own way to a full worldview bound devotion to the work of the Father, almighty, maker of heaven and earth. The challenge I faced at Princeton Seminary, dominated as it was by Barthian thought, came to focus in my work at St. Michael's through the always prescient help of my advisor and mentor, Herbert W. Richardson. He pointed me in the direction of the Swedish theologian Gustaf Wingren and his extensive work on the eclipse of creation in modern theology, which became the focus of my doctoral dissertation.

Once my attention turned to business after I left the academy, I discontinued doing the many things that keep professors busy, but I never stopped thinking about the significance of creation in Christian thought. It has been a theme that has continued to weave its way through reflections on many things. Business CEOs do not have a tradition on the order of a last lecture, but I find it worthwhile again to review my intellectual autobiography in order once more to make a concluding statement about what I continue firmly to believe is the importance of a strong understanding of "creation" in Christian thought and practice. This book, *Creation: An Introduction to Christian Thought*, is my effort at a "final lecture."

CHAPTER 1

Introduction and a Statement of the Problem

I HAVE CALLED MY treatment of the topic of creation "Creation as an Introduction to Christian Thought." The reader may notice that I do not speak of the "doctrine of creation." The reader may also notice that I do not refer very often to the "theology of creation." Though such references may be made appropriately, I have chosen not to make them generally in this book because I believe that they distract from one of my main concerns. "Creation" does not function in much Christian thought as it should because the function of *analyzing* creation reality has, in the modern period, been handed over to what is called "science," where it is analyzed within the framework of "secular thought."

Some theologians have ignored creation knowingly and deliberately.[1] Moreover the mainline Christian community slipped into something similar to what the dominant elite culture churned up, with the exception of minimal, nonoffensive morality and therapeutic recommendations. In his 2005 book Christian Smith calls this minimalist attitude "Moralistic Therapeutic Deism."[2] Moreover, as one writer has put it: "The Old Testament is dying,"[3] which is the primary location of the creation narrative and the seat of the Torah, as well as of the Wisdom and prophetic writings that are dependent for their sense on the Pentateuch. We are to "love God above all and our neighbor as ourselves," but we eclipse and tend to ignore the why

---

1. Hendry, *Theology of Nature*, 18–20.
2. Smith, *Soul Searching*.
3. Strawn, *Old Testament Is Dying*.

and the how of doing that as outlined in considerable detail by the Elder Testament.[4]

As a person trained entirely from my first years to my last (when I reached the age of thirty) in specifically Christian educational institutions, "creation" was implicitly functioning in my educational world. "Creation" wasn't just a doctrine studied in church, or in theology classes in the schools I attended. It was in fact functioning as the object matter of study in every discipline in which students were being instructed. More importantly, "creation" was functioning not only as the object matter (today many would say "subject matter" instead) but also as *the vantage point from which most of the instructors I was privileged to have* (especially at Calvin University from 1964 to 1968) were discussing, analyzing, and teaching their various fields of expertise. The handing over of this enterprise to non-Christian institutions was typically not considered an option in the view of the educational world in which I lived and moved about.

In much of the educational world in which many Christians operate and have been educated, that privilege was not the case and did not exist. However, in Christian schools "creation" represented, and represents, not only the object matter being investigated, but also the set of formative influences that controlled how these various object matters were represented to the student.

"Creation" is the reality we all investigate in the educational enterprise as a whole, which is what I, therefore, call "Christian ontology." But it is also the pre-theoretical vantage point from which the investigations in all the disciplines are controlled. The latter I would, therefore, call "Christian epistemology." Together these two constitute "Christian philosophy," which I take to be the comprehensive view of things that should found and undergird the entire Christian academic enterprise, informing even the most elementary levels on which the education of young children should take place within the Christian community of faith. Christian education at all levels is one of the first arenas in which faith comes to life. It is truly one of the primary areas in which an all-encompassing kingdom vision (Elder and Younger Testaments included) is executed. I will elaborate on this by personal testimony shortly.

---

4. I have chosen throughout to use Rabbi David Zaslow's designation of the OT as the Elder Testament and his designation of the NT as the Younger Testament. See his *Jesus: First Century Rabbi*.

Introduction and a Statement of the Problem

In the Christian educational world "creation" was always there behaviorally and formatively in a way in which it was not, and even is not now, for many Christian believers being educated in public and secular institutions. The habit of leaving it to "science," or to "public education," or to the "secular academy" is a hurdle for "creation faith." In Christian schools students are not habituated or continuously exposed to that way of thinking, except in books and in the writings of others.

That situation of a cultural barrier being the case for many in other settings, "Christian faith" has necessarily become associated with other matters, especially with the way of salvation (often, without creation, narrowly conceived as a "personal relation with Jesus" or what happens to one's "soul" when one dies). Or it is associated (narrowly I would say) with the church as an ecclesiastical institution in society. Or it is associated with Christian doctrine, or with some other dimension of life in the world dealt with in the academy by the discipline of theology. There is then "learning" on the one hand and "faith" on the other. There is then "science" on the one hand and "religion" on the other. There are thus two magnitudes that are essentially separate, or maybe (and even worse, because neither magnitude is understood properly) complementary. Unfortunately this arrangement of things fails to take full advantage of what "creation" (and its location in the Elder Testament) in the Christian faith has to offer.

It is because of this central phenomenon (among many additional matters to be discussed later) that "creation" has been underplayed or eclipsed in much modern Christian thought and practice. In some Christian traditions it has been marginalized. In some it has been replaced and/or, in yet others, fundamentalistically redefined or constricted. The eclipse of creation, to which I will devote considerable space in this book, has been variable in both form and degree. Eighty years ago already the Swedish theologian Gustaf Wingren wrote extensively about the flight from creation in both modern thought as well as in modern theology. In fact Wingren wrote a significant book with exactly that title.[5] To his contributions on this topic I will refer frequently. In addition, in recent years one can notice a large flurry of new books devoted to an exploration of creation, in part at least because it has been so neglected, underplayed, and narrowly conceived in the past.

Common Christian thinking about faith in addition to much modern Christian theology focus on Jesus Christ and human salvation alone as the

---

5. Wingren, *Flight from Creation*.

Creation as an Introduction to Christian Thought

essence of Christian faith. The focus on the Younger Testament's "no creed but Christ" persists even in discussions that intend special consideration of science and its relation to Christian faith. I am strongly inclined to call this obsession "Christological Unitarianism." God is not one, but Three in One. We believe, as professed by the historic Christian faith, that God is Father, Son, and Holy Spirit, with the Father first and his work witnessed to first in the Elder Testament, which appears first in the canon of the Bible. Order of right teaching requires that all fully Christian faith claims begin there, especially those that focus on the integration of faith and learning. Just as we generally tend to call the neglect of Christ and human salvation among many founding fathers of the American Republic "Unitarianism" and "Deism," so focus on Jesus and our salvation has become a new "Christomonistic Unitarianism." This latter phenomenon has emerged in Europe among followers of Karl Barth and in the United States among so-called fundamentalists.

Creation is, I claim in contrast to these exclusively Christ-centered emphases, the major introduction to Christian thought. It is first and foremost the everything that is, visible and invisible; in Scripture it is the "heavens and the earth." It is the reality in which every creature of God lives and has ever lived. But "creation" is also the *story about that reality* of the cosmos that we find in Scripture, where we find it (no surprise) at the very beginning of the book, in which (no surprise) the entire "Elder" part or Testament was placed before the "Younger" part or Testament. The canon begins at the beginning. That specific compilation even took place *after* the Younger Testament was composed/compiled, whose central and main theme was Jesus Christ; no creed but Christ. The canonizers knew full well what they were doing; they were noticeably warding off any form of the downplaying of creation, called Gnosticism in the ancient world and Marcionism in the early church.[6] Finally, the creation story is so prominent that it is the most mentioned theme in the entire text of the Elder and the Younger Testaments.

It must be said again and again and strongly that we do not, therefore, have "two" books of revelation here, as one Protestant confession, The Belgic Confession, seems to suggest. This confession is on this point significantly less Protestant than most other confessions of the Reformation.

---

6. See Jonas, *Gnostic Religion*. According to Eric Voegelin, modern versions have also appeared. See his *Science, Politics, and Gnosticism*. Finally, Marcion was the second-century thinker who alleged that the God of the OT was a different God than the God of the NT.

Introduction and a Statement of the Problem

I emphasize that because the so-called book of creation must, of course, be read. What it reveals is not self-evident in a fallen world. What it means is not mirrored onto the *tabula rasa* of our minds. Thus the so-called book of creation cannot be read by, in, and of itself, but must be read by the light of the "other" book. We do not have here the "book of nature," readable adequately by the light of science or natural reason alone, and then in addition the book of the Bible, which, so to speak, "completes" the job with some supranatural add-ons.

As we shall see again and again in the work of John Calvin, the "book of Scripture" must be used as "spectacles"[7] for the right reading of anything and everything. This includes the reading of Scripture itself, because it has to be read having already been accepted in the loving embrace of it at the native level.[8] The need for biblical perspective is also necessary for an overall right reading of the so-called book of creation. From the epistemic point of view, Calvin at his best, in the genuine reforming of thought after the medieval period, was a radical bibliocentrist. In some of his writings that went through numerous editions over the years, one can detect remnants of the Scholastic-metaphysical and Renaissance views of natural reason, though it is significant that not a single mention is made of Thomas Aquinas in Calvin's entire corpus. But where, to use the words of Karl Barth, Calvin has turned the corner and climbed a high mountain,[9] as is evident in book 1 of the final 1559 edition of the *Institutes of the Christian Religion*, he is clear about the centrality of the "spectacles" of the Scriptures. Without those glasses, we are truly "bleary eyed men with weak vision," no matter what we're looking at.[10]

Apart from the story about creation in Scripture (a story not shared by all), there is, of course, the reality of creation itself and accordingly the many stories about it that the reality itself has called forth among various peoples all over the world. All of the stories, of course, come from and after the realities to which they refer. They are not just stories borrowed from other peoples and then reworked.[11] Historical science within the disci-

---

7. Calvin, *Institutes* 1.5.14.
8. Vander Goot, *Interpreting the Bible*.
9. Cf. Barth, *Revolutionary Theology in the Making*, 101.
10. Calvin, *Institutes* 1.6.1–2.
11. Greenblatt, *Rise and Fall of Adam and Eve*, and countless others on Israel's creation story as coming out of the context of textually older Babylonian mythic stories.

pline of theology has been obsessed with the latter approach of historical sourcing.

By contrast the reality of what actually happened was itself powerful, mysterious, inescapable, bearing in on all peoples of the world as an unavoidable and inescapable *force majeure*. This can be abundantly illustrated through common or similar creation stories that were each quite independent (historically) efforts to ascertain and remember and live into that reality of reality. This is especially true of mythic stories that had no historical connection with one another. No particular credit here to human beings in their fallen condition but no doubt a marvelous credit to the Creator's faithfulness to what he had created and then preserved, in spite of the habits of his creatures to undo and abuse it. As Paul says, "the Gentiles do by nature what the law requires,"[12] no story or book to help them. Coming from the apostle of "salvation by grace alone," this is Paul's praise of God, of course, not of some minimal credit to the gentiles. There was also the non-Hebrew and virtuous Melchizedek, mentioned in Gen 14 and again in Heb 5–7. Similarly, Hammurabi's moral code bears striking resemblance to the Hebrew Torah.

The cosmos has its own in-built karma, so to speak, and we could go on and on about what imprints that has left on all peoples of the human race. We could go on and on pointing such matters out, searching for historical connections among the various myths; or we, contra the apostle Paul, could end up with a discussion of the confused and confusing concept of "common grace." Invariably this would deflect attention from the power of the work of God's hands to some preexisting quality of righteousness possessed by all human beings.[13]

In any case, the reference of all things created to the one who is above and beyond is thus to be seen in all things, at all times, and among all peoples. I call this referencing, this push, in all and every area of life "religion." All peoples seek a resting place, a point of orientation, an ultimate explanation for the why and wherefore of things past, present, and forevermore. This all-encompassing basis or foundation of creation is found in God, just as the inescapable reference to and push in things toward him as the object

---

12. Rom 2:14.

13. Grace alone is supposed to be freely given, not already possessed to some degree, generally speaking, by everyone. We need to clean up our theological rhetoric in many places, but this equivocation on the term "grace" in the use of the term "common grace" is certainly an extremely important lapse in logic. As we all know, lapses in logic create many confusions in discourse.

of ultimate concern is present in religion first and foremost. Most peoples of the past, like the Israelites, experienced life as religion in and through all the various centers of identity and initiative in their lives. Religion was and is the whole thing. For example, the Indian philosopher Avinash Chandra has made a strong case that among Asian cultures this view is widely held.[14] In his extensive characterization of religion, he lays out in detail the picture of the significant difference between the West and the Asian world on this matter. Chandra says, "Spiritual experience should form the basis of our knowledge of the universe: a vision of unity that is not opposed to any partial knowledge (such as genuine scientific knowledge) but rather integrates them all."[15]

A. RELIGION'S MARGINALIZATION AND SILENT DIMINISHMENT

The story of most religions begins with this inescapable reality, as it does in the Hebrew and Christian Scriptures. Particularly in the development of Western Christianity, however, the great crisis of religion's marginalization and minimalization emerged. By "marginalization" I am referring to a gradual process of seeing religion as less than the whole foundation and meaning of all things. Gradually religion came to be seen as a *piece of life* rather than as the foundation in, and spiritive referencing of, all things to their divine, transcendent source.

1. Dualism in Plato and Aristotle

On the model of the Greek and Roman philosophers, it was thought that all reality is reducible to its material aspects plus the idea, or "form," or essence. These then were conceived as two sides, according to Plato, "two worlds," arranged hierarchically from the lower and mundane to the higher and ideal. The latter, higher and ideal, is associated with the so-called noetic cosmos, which is the "logos" itself. The unfortunate use in the Aramaic world of Jesus of this latter term, "logos," in the prologue to the Gospel of John has created remarkable confusion in the history of Christianity. The apostle Paul already experienced a sharp chasm between Jerusalem

---

14. See the fine characterization of religion in Chandra, *Scientist and the Saint*, 19–50.
15. Chandra, *Scientist and the Saint*, 41.

and Athens when he visited with the philosophers there (Acts 17:16–34). Accordingly, it is useful on this point to compare the Logos Speculations of both Origen and Philo of Alexandria. How did the church fathers get there from the Hebrew Yeshua of Nazareth, his preaching and teaching, and from the faithful ministry of Paul?

In early church history, the distinction between the ideal and the real gradually came to be conceived as a separation. The lesser of the two was designated the material world, the "*ho cosmos, ho horatus.*" This was the beginning in Western Christianity of referring to the lesser material side as "nature," or in the case of the person, "the body." The other, more important and "eternal" side was called the "spiritual," or "supranatural," and in the case of the person, "the soul." I shall contend throughout our discussion here that nothing could be further from and more foreign to the Jewish and Christian faiths than these Gnostic Greek and pagan ideas. Eventually, within Catholicism there developed a more subtle way of expressing this theme: in the motif of "nature and grace," the latter formed and "completed" nature.[16]

Emerging Western Christianity could have done better if it had kept its eyes on the Scriptures of Yeshua (Joshua), who was a Jew. Of course, more than likely we ourselves would have been caught up in the trends of the times and given dominance to Greco-Roman culture as it influenced the emergence and spread of Christianity. Rather than seeing this influence as a diminishment of the message, the modern classicist Werner Jaeger considered this development (joining Jerusalem and Athens) the best of all possible worlds. Christianity, he thought, needed a culture and the Greco-Roman world needed a viable religion that had gone beyond ancient Greek polytheism and the later, Roman "Caesar-is-God."[17] In the 1930s Jaeger had fled Nazi Germany and resettled in the United States, where he became known for his studies of the classics both at the University of Chicago and later at Harvard University.

---

16. Niebuhr, *Christ and Culture*, 116–41, and the reference to this view as "Christ Above Culture."

17. Runner, *Walking in the Way*, xiv–xix. At Harvard University Runner studied with Werner Jaeger. Later at the Free University of Amsterdam Runner developed a much more antithetical view of the relationship of Christianity and Greek culture.

2. Religion and the Church

Another significant and highly unfortunate result of the diminishment of religion's comprehensiveness within Christianity was the identification of religion with the church as an ecclesiastical institution. This occurred not long after the apostolic period along with efforts to view Peter as the first pope, a revision of history that is questionable and quite unfortunate. This conflation of "church" and "religion" is a confusion that has persisted to this very day. "Church" is the first thing people are inclined to think of when the word "religion" gets mentioned. Also, when in the United States we speak of the "separation of church and state," the vast majority of the population assumes this means that religion and the public square need to be kept separate. There is little appreciation of the glaring equivocation on the terms "church" and "religion." In any case religion's meaning and the range of its significance and application became drastically narrowed to one social and cultural institution.

Subsequently, as a result of this narrowing, the ecclesiastical institution in turn began to think increasingly *expansively* about itself, its task, and its authority in human society. In a pattern of mission creep it began to assume that its institutional task should be extended into every area of life. As a result of this expansion, the institutional church began regarding itself as first and foremost among the institutions of society, the *major* institution alongside of the state, which since antiquity had been the overarching kingdom, empire, or *polis*.

Parallel to this, the discipline of theology came to be viewed as the overall discipline of Christian perspective, the "queen" of the sciences. All too frequently we hear a Christian perspective on some cultural matter referred to as the "theology" of that matter: so we have "the theology of science," or "the theology of immigration," or the "theology of the family" surfacing at one time or another. In addition, the church saw itself as also needing a "Caesar" of sorts. And, guess what, they got a "pope" for the *polis* of God, a figurehead who wears robes like a king and carries on his head something vaguely resembling a crown.

Next in this development the church made claims to be "higher" than and "superordinate" to the state, not just equal to it. And, finally, by this totalizing and integralizing way of thinking, inherent in the nature of religion though *not* in the nature of one social institution among others, from the time of Constantine to the tenth century, a constant back and forth emerged over whether the church or the state was supreme. These conflicts are well known as the "Caesaro-Papist" controversies. Ever since in the West it has become increasingly difficult to distinguish clearly between religion on the one hand and the institutional church on the other, each term evoking meanings that belong to the other. The same confusion emerged in the discipline of "theology," which all too often came to mean "Christian religious perspective." These confusions have caused immense damage in Western thought about what religion is as well as deep confusion about what the work of the discipline of theology should be. What is forgotten much of the time is that theology is only one discipline among a host of others.

This was only the beginning. When the domination of the ecclesiastical sphere by the Roman Catholic Church was broken by the Reformation, all hell broke loose. Not only did the Catholic Church come into conflict with the empire, even in its Holy Roman form, but suddenly the "ecclesiastical" side of the conflict was splintered into multiple and varying forms of the church, with each vying for dominance among the others. The end result was the hideous "Wars of Religion" of the sixteenth and seventeenth centuries in Europe.

The "Wars of Religion" that included the Thirty Years War and the Eighty Years War were finally resolved in the Treaty of Westphalia of 1648. In it the actual military conflicts among the various church groups (Catholics, Lutherans, Calvinists) were brought to an end with the formula "*cuius regio, euis religio,*" meaning "whose region, his religion." In practice this formula meant that the church affiliation of the region's ruler was to become the governmentally favored "religion" or church of the region. Where the ruler was Catholic, the state church of that region became Catholic. Where the ruler was Lutheran or Calvinist, the new nation-state favored church of that region would become Lutheran or Calvinist.[18] Once again here the concepts "church" and "religion" are used equivocally.

One cannot overestimate the damage done in the history of modern thought and the confusions created in society by this glaring equivocation! The phenomenon of a state favored church lasted well into the twentieth century in Europe. And, most destructively, the idea of the "separation of church and state" in the United States came to mean that religion and the public square should not, and do not have, *anything* to do with one another. Logical errors can have far-reaching consequences.

---

18. Wikipedia, "European Wars of Religion."

3. The First Enlightenment

Out of this nightmare in the history of Western Christianity the turn away from religion (and not just from the churches) and the serious narrowing of the scope of religion began to take place. The leaders of this modern development were the thinkers of the first Enlightenment, who regarded religion as the cause of the murderous Wars of Religion during which eight million people died. They raised up "reason" as the solution to the problem because it could be unaffiliated with religion in any sense and therefore be seen as "objective." Philosophy and science uttered only what was reasonable and thus true. Reason and religion became separated from one another, at least on the deliberate and self-conscious level. In reality, of course it was not possible to box in religion, not for anyone, not even for those such as the Deists who thought they could do so by stripping away the "miraculous" sides of the Christian faith.

Reason became first and foremost what makes good plain sense. The extraordinary, the so-called supranatural, claims of religion were discarded. Newton and Locke did this in England, and later in the United States Thomas Jefferson followed their example. They could not be judged as non-Christians, but they purged Christianity of the extraordinary, the unthinkable, and the unreasonable. This in turn played into the rise of modern scientific thinking.

The arena in which reason operated center stage came to be called "science," true knowledge, or truth, pure and simple. Witness even today how public media stands aghast when someone claims "not to *believe* in science." Reason sets aside everything except those easily managed aspects of things such as their count, their ability to be circumscribed with number, the space they occupy, the mass and the energy that is exerted on them and by them via gravity. With this focus it is thought that the scientist can find the truth about things as they are in themselves.

It also came to be thought that these abstractive methods and measurements apply everywhere in the universe. They are principles of continuity that apply universally. Many among these Enlightenment thinkers came to be known as "Physiocrats," and carried their ideas forward by wielding their power in politics as well. Consider for example the dubious use of a *mathematical* term "equality" in the *political* realm of the state and the vast repercussions that would have in the future formation of liberalism and the idea of the social contract state. The so-called natural sciences emerged as dominant and as models for all science, which had become for most of these thinkers the "mirror of nature," pure and simple. Many Christians began to think that even the Scriptures are populated with that kind of knowledge and truth.[19]

4. The Second Enlightenment: Immanuel Kant

There was a very significant second development of the Enlightenment view of reason and religion in the work of Immanuel Kant. He is well known for the claim that he put "limits on science to make room for faith." To him this meant that religion operates within the "boundaries of mere reason." To secure a place for "religion" Kant thoroughly transformed the idea of scientific "objectivity." There is raw material out there, according to Kant, but the mind itself has in-built ways of organizing, and these ways are universal. They are "transcendental" among human beings. On the sensory, perceptual level, there are, according to Kant, the "forms of sensibility." These he identified as "space" and "time," and they are the two prominent ways in which humans universally order the raw data of experience.

Understanding, according to Kant's way of thinking, then takes over and further arranges the raw space-time data using its in-built and *a priori* categories, such as cause and effect, or unity and multiplicity, in order to make coherent, rational sense of things. The so-called objectivity of reason comes from the universality of the *mind's* constitution among human beings, *not* from the thing out there, the so-called *Ding an sich*.

Given Kant's turn to the human subject of knowledge, "objectivity" does not come from something out there, or from some "thing in itself." The "thing in itself" in essence remains unknown. The human subject, structurally the same everywhere, in effect constitutes the object and thus does not mirror it as given raw material (nature). The object becomes the subject. Oh what fun and bizarredom this portends, especially in the twenty-first century. The way things are becomes identified with the human subject's positivization of them. Everything can now become a social construction rather than a natural, common-sense reality.

So long as human beings do not use religious beliefs as scientific concepts in which the forms of sensibility and the categories of the understanding are assumed to apply, they become extremely important in lending "meaning" and "value" to human life, according to Kant. "The moral thing to do" turns into "let me tell you about my feelings and values." For there

---

19. Frei, *Eclipse of Biblical Narrative*, 86–154.

Introduction and a Statement of the Problem

to be an orderly and livable culture and society, human beings are enabled to create "meanings" through the "pure, practical reason." Meanings thus effectuated are used erroneously if they are assumed to have objective significance, i.e., to have the status of scientific truths, although Kant had put limits on that idea too in order to make room for faith, religion, and other meaning giving operations of the practical reason.

The fallacy of using "meaning" as if it had scientific truth significance is called by Kant the "metaphysical fallacy," i.e., the application of space-time forms and the categories of the understanding to matters that transcend the possibility of being given to us in empirical experience. The world as it is in itself, the so-called *Ding an sich* world, as well as the transcendent, as traditionally understood, are in principle unknowable. Those who claim to know them are really only absolutizing their own opinions. A significant role has been preserved for religion and ethics, but they have definitely been put in their place by being edged out of the domain of speaking truth.

Kant goes even further to suggest that among human beings the main meaning giving principles of human practice are God, freedom, and immortality. Kant calls these the "principles of the pure practical reason." In effect Kant claims that all religions and systems of morality make life livable as human beings universally create meanings around essentially these three deep structure schemas. To live a meaningful life, human beings universally project some story about the origin of all things by a divine being. During year-opening ceremonies at the University of Kønigsberg, Kant participated in the processionals, but when the line came to the chapel, Kant excused himself and went elsewhere. Since he did not believe that there was a god, he felt conscience-bound not to pretend that he did in public.[20]

In addition, according to Kant, most try their best to create some sense of what evil is and some sense of the remedy for it. There is the astonishing fact of human freedom, that human beings are responsible earthlings. Finally most human beings project meaning by advancing some understanding of a life to come, in which this life is vindicated in some way or another, so that life is not experienced as meaningless in the here and now. So long as human beings do not view these beliefs, meanings, and values as objectively true, they stand as important stabilizers in human culture and society. Kant had thus made a prominent place for religion and values in life so long as its beliefs were not treated as scientific or "objective," or so

---

20. This anecdote was related by one of my professors in a 1967 class.

long as these beliefs were not used to challenge science, in Kant's sense of the term.

This new Kantian, Enlightenment scheme became known as "categorical complementarism." There are then the two realms of rational knowledge and human praxis. These two can stand alongside of one another because they perform essentially *different* functions, "truth" being achieved by the former and meaningfulness and value by the latter. How often does one not hear that science tells us "how" things work and the "religions" tell us about the "why." Oh how fun this has become in modern centuries when even Christians try to paste together worldviews and myths that are essentially incompatible. I think in particular of the hybrid of "theistic evolutionism," about which I have to say more in subsequent chapters. One might consider too the rise some decades ago of "liberation-read Marxist-theology."

In any case, we might say that in Kant the "object" becomes the "subject," and the "thing in itself" the unknowable. This way of thinking would become much more prevalent as time went on in the nineteenth and twentieth centuries. Perhaps to interpret Kant with charity since he completed his system of thought toward the end of his life, we might wonder if this was Kant's own personal way of acknowledging the complex *mystery* of it all. In any case, religion and beliefs were "put in their place" by Kant. In the wake of his pronouncements we end not with reason within the bounds of religion but with religion within the bounds of reason alone. In the subsequent centuries God is gradually marginalized or reduced to a personal preference, or as Nietzsche would aver later in the nineteenth century, God was gradually put to death by us. Could we be any further from the profession of faith as found in Acts 17:28 which declares that "in God we live and move and have our being"? Could we have moved any further away from the understanding that "all of life is religion"?

B. CONTEMPORARY RESPONSES ATTEMPTING TO RECOVER "LIFE IS RELIGION"

In the twentieth century a deep sense of resistance emerged to the marginalizing of God in modern, Western, secular culture. In Protestantism "Radical Orthodoxy" sought a correction in a push toward wholeness and comprehensiveness in religion. In Catholicism it reemerged in what is called "integralism," i.e., the idea that the whole of society needs to be ordered under the dome of the church. It has also been the case in non-Western

Introduction and a Statement of the Problem

religions that many preach that the whole of life has its foundation in religion. In short, that life is religion.

1. A Personal Note

I was fortunate myself to attend a Protestant university in which many of my teachers assumed the latter point of view. Some said all learning, in every discipline, is "faith seeking understanding." Others said, similarly, that reason really always functions within the bounds of religion, that in effect beliefs form the context of even thought. But the most prophetic of my teachers simply reiterated frequently that "life is religion."[21] The push back against the Western separation of religion from politics, education, and the other areas of sociocultural life has inevitably emerged. To many it has become clear that so-called public schools are in fact as immersed in worldview perspectives as are so-called private and parochial schools. One can see a similar view in the work of Richard John Neuhaus and the founding of *First Things*, a journal of the Institute on Religion and Public Life. Also from the point of view of the traditions of far Eastern religions and culture many have noticed an increasing secularization in the West. In the United States a similar view may be found among Native American thinkers. As our discussion here moves forward, I will cite two prominent examples of these patterns of new worldview thinking.[22]

In my introduction of Christian creation thought, I wish also to describe how the "life is religion" view developed in my own biography. This did not happen intellectually, as it does in few people. To that intellectual task and activity I turned later, when I came to embrace in the academic world that religion is the comprehensive context of all things, including scholarly thought. At that point I was not studying theology but rather philosophy and classics.

All thought, scientific or not, has its foundation outside of itself. Even trust in the power and authority of thought comes from somewhere else than from thought itself. If it comes to "trust in the power of thought," there couldn't be a worse choice. For sure the foundation cannot be proven undeniably in the logical, rational sense. At best the foundation may show itself to be warranted. The "life is religion" foundation is formed early in a

---

21. Cf. Vander Goot, *Life Is Religion*.
22. Chandra, *Scientist and the Saint*. Also see Deloria, *God Is Red*.

person's life through basic and simple experiences.[23] I shall try briefly to describe my own pre-academic formation below.

I was born in the Netherlands (Friesland) in 1946. My parents, my sister, and I immigrated to the United States in 1948. Because my father had an uncle in Grand Rapids, Michigan, we settled there. Within a few months we settled into the lunch bucket side of Grand Rapids, in the Dutch immigrant ghetto on the southwest side of the city. My mother gave birth not only to me but to my basic Christian faith as well. She had herself been a member of the *Geformeerde Kerk* of the Netherlands. However, she was also deeply shaped by the Oxford Movement when it entered the Netherlands in the 1930s. She was a pious, kind, and caregiving Christian for her two children. My father had also become a member of the same denomination when he married my mother. But he was no hero of the faith. He was rather a fiercely hard-working Friesian, showing us that one couldn't get anywhere without putting oneself into one's work. People create their own identities, selves, and names in the course of what they do in life. My mother was my faith hero, and my father was my work hero.

We read the Bible and prayed at meal times. We prayed again at bedtime. We associated with immigrants in the nearby community who had the same habits. My mother and our neighbors encouraged my father to join the local Christian Reformed Church. From out of a Christian home I went to a Christian church in the neighborhood. In the early 1950s there was still a Dutch service as well as an English language service at the church we joined. We attended both. My father enjoyed the Dutch service in particular because the minister, Ymen Peter De Jong, was a Friesian character whom one could meet on Saturday afternoons at the local Dutch import store, Vander Veen's, owned by a Friesian too. The minister occasionally invited my father to the parsonage for some herbal remedies for his stomach ulcers. During those visits my father also enjoyed a nice shot of whiskey that the pastor produced in his basement distillery. The immigrant parishioners called Grandville Avenue Church "YP's throne."

Another important influence was the educational setting of my early years. Naturally my parents sent my sister and me to the local Christian school, immediately behind Grandville Avenue Church. This school was a private Christian school, organized by Reformed parents through a parent-controlled entity called "Christian Schools International." When not at home or in church, I was with my friends and playmates in and about this

---

23. Cf. Sweetman, *Tracing the Lines*.

Southwest Christian School. The playground was our neighborhood park, or an extension of our own backyards. The bulk of my free time was spent not just in school, but also in play and association with my fellow classmates, who lived in the general neighborhood of YP's throne.

My pastors at Grandville Avenue Church became my intellectual heroes, both in the arena of work but also in faith and thinking about the faith. The person who stood out in particular was my pastor in the early sixties, as I made my way from junior high at Southwest Christian to Grand Rapids Christian High, the CSI secondary school in Grand Rapids. I read my first theological books there on the advice of my pastor, John Henry Piersma. He suggested Cornelius Van Til's *The New Modernism* and *Defense of the Faith*. Van Til had developed a conservative Presbyterian version of Dutch Neo-Calvinism. He emphasized that all thought is borne along with and upon "presuppositions."

As I entered what was then called Calvin College (now Calvin University) for my undergraduate education, I fell in with philosophers. I decided to major in philosophy and classics, even though I was registered in the college's pre-seminary program. When my favorite philosopher, H. Evan Runner, passionately proclaimed that "life is religion," my reaction, coming out of the environment that I had, was, "that's a great way of putting it!"

It is exactly here that one can see the major point I have brought to the fore in my introduction: in every context of my life up to that point (church, home, and school), I was surrounded by and embedded in a Christian religious environment. That is how I had been *formed*. I had been formed for years in the course of my pre-critical and pre-analytical primary experience. It was only natural that I brought that with me in every discipline I studied, though I preferred philosophy because it was the most comprehensive and all-encompassing of the academic subjects. I quickly realized that when intellectual capacities are set in motion, Christian faith formation leads invariably to a life vision or worldview. I was moving from being formed by Christian faith-shaped environments to a beginning intellectual grasp of things, and then finally on to the academic enterprise with all of its many areas of interest.

2. Secular Theology

Theology is an academic discipline among others in the academy. Its subject matter is sacred texts, the church, worship, Christian creeds, and

Christian teachings and their history. One can approach that subject matter *with faith formation in place*. However, it is also possible to approach that subject matter with a starting point other than Christian faith formation in place. In effect it can be approached from a secular stance. It is even possible to approach the subject matter with skepticism vis-à-vis the Christian faith. There is little recognition of these complex cross-currents in modern Christian thought. Theology in itself is not necessarily a good and safe place.

Particularly in the modern period, uninformed "reason" is believed to be the proper approach to truth in any discipline, including theology. As argued above, modern believers in reason understood it as some neutral or objective stance that stood above the battle of the church affiliations and religious beliefs such as these that had turned into the Wars of Religion. The champions of autonomous, objective reason relied for their claims of credibility entirely on supposedly impersonal methods. They claimed thus to have set aside all assumptions with regard to content. That theology has a "sacred" subject matter did *not* imply that the discipline would be executed from a Christian faith perspective. Biblical theologians especially fed this "neutral" or "objective" approach into the discipline of theology.

A prime example of this appears in a small volume published in 1994 by the Biblical Archaeology Society. Two prominent scholars of religion write articles about their work. In one of the first articles authored by Marcus Borg, he tells the reader that he is employed at a state-funded university and that thus "it is inappropriate to approach the study of Jesus with specifically Christian presuppositions or with his significance for Christian faith in mind."[24] Despite this, Borg immediately claims personally to be a Christian.

When I read this and the rest of the book that follows along the same lines, my immediate response is: "Who's getting the *truth*?" Are Borg's students in a state university where "scholarship and teaching" are being done with an approach that tries to eliminate all subjective elements, even though that is now considered impossible according to the modern philosophy of science? Or is the full truth only to be found in the church, where Borg worships and where his own wife is the priest?[25] Either Jesus lived, "was crucified, died and was buried, . . . and on the third day rose again from the

---

24. Patterson et al., *Search for Jesus*, 38.
25. Patterson et al., *Search for Jesus*, 37–38.

Introduction and a Statement of the Problem

dead, and ascended into heaven," or *he did not*. How can Borg's students be getting the *truth* if these beliefs/facts are being left out?

Can there be and should there not be the integration of faith and learning in the academy, and would it not use warranted Christian beliefs in the process? Or is the *truth* that which lacks the inclusion of these beliefs? The latter has become the fate of theology and religious studies in the modern, secular university as a result of efforts to make these disciplines qualify as true sciences.

In the Enlightenment reaction to the Wars of Religion, faith claims came to be subjected to the test of "what is purely reasonable." As we see clearly from this case, *the subject matter of theology does not guarantee the proper treatment or construal of the subject matter*. And it is exactly this that is often confused in the use of the term "theology" itself, as well as in the term "religious studies." It is also deliberately set aside or forgotten in the modern study of various texts and in the historical critical disciplines.

Another clear example of this implicit confusion is the theology of Rudolf Bultmann, who tried to demonstrate that a genuinely critical and analytical theology in the modern period understands that the whole content of faith is myth, values, and wishful thinking. This was no problem for Bultmann's own personal Christian faith. As a Lutheran, he did not believe that reason and the disciplines can or should be "faith seeking understanding." In fact for Bultmann "faith seeking understanding" is an intellectual form of "works righteousness" that seeks to make faith easier than an unwarranted leap into the dark night of the soul.[26] As Paul Tyson has claimed in his intriguing book on Christian theology, "historical-critical theology created the death blow to western Christian theology."[27]

The subject matter of theology (beliefs, the Bible, the church as an ecclesiastical institution, etc.) can only be studied properly and productively in the academy by a person who has already long before been formed and shaped existentially, pre-theoretically, by the Bible's world. The Bible as a subject matter of theology needs to be treated with tender, loving care! It is indeed a divine book, but it is also at once thoroughly human with fragile components. Without the exercise of tender, loving care, theology has become a bundle of tools used to disassemble the subject matter and chip away at it with critical instruments to get at what is "literally" true. By "literally true" is meant what corresponds to the facts as a particular

26. Bultmann, "New Testament and Mythology," 3.
27. Tyson, *Christian Theology of Science*, 143.

science sees them, and especially how modern history or modern literary criticism see them. There is no guarantee in the discipline of theology that it will, because of the nature of its subject matter, go in the right direction. One has first to love the Bible to be able to analyze and explain its meaning productively. When this attitude of affirmation is absent or academically, abstractively suspended from the outset, theology can become its own wrecking ball.

John Calvin put it all this way. We are all like bleary-eyed persons in our broken condition. For a proper knowledge of God, the world, and ourselves, we need to put on a pair of good glasses. That pair of fitting glasses is the "spectacles of the Scriptures" for Calvin. Theology is a science that studies the realities of faith, Christian creeds and teachings, the church, etc., among other things. To see those matters rightly, one needs first to have put on the "spectacles of the Scriptures." To study Scripture one needs Scripture. Calvin's words in this context are worthy of full citation. After concluding in chapter 5, section 14, book 1 of the *Institutes* that "the manifestation of God in nature speaks to us in vain," Calvin begins chapter 6 saying:

> That brightness which is borne in upon the eyes of all men both in heaven and on earth is more than enough to withdraw all support from men's ingratitude—just as God, to involve the human race in the same guild, sets forth to us without exception his presence portrayed in his creatures. Despite this, it is needful that another and better help be added to direct us aright to the very Creator of the universe . . . . For because he saw the minds of all men tossed and agitated, after he chose the Jews as his very own flock, he fenced them about that they might not sink into oblivion as others had. With good reason he holds by the same means in the pure knowledge of himself since otherwise even those who seem to stand firm before all others would soon melt away. Just as old bleary-eyed men and those with weak vision, if you thrust before them a most beautiful volume, even if they recognize it to be some sort of writing, yet can scarcely construe two words, but with the aid of spectacles will begin to read distinctly; so Scripture, gathering up the otherwise confused knowledge of God in our minds, having dispersed our dullness clearly shows us the true God. . . . There is no doubt that Adam, Noah, Abraham, and the rest of the patriarchs with this assistance penetrated to the intimate knowledge of him that in a way distinguished them from unbelievers. I am not yet speaking of the proper doctrine of faith whereby they

had been illuminated unto the hope of eternal life. For, that they might pass from death to life, it was necessary to recognize God not only as Creator but also as Redeemer, for undoubtedly they arrived at both from the Word. First in order came the kind of knowledge by which one is permitted to grasp that God founded and governs the universe. . . . But because we have not yet come to the fall of the world and the corruption of nature, I shall now forego a discussion of the remedy. . . . Here I shall discuss only how we should learn from Scripture that God, the Creator of the universe, can by sure marks be distinguished from all the throng of feigned gods. Nevertheless, all things will tend to this end, that that God, the Artificer of the universe, is made manifest to us in Scripture.[28]

To get at the conundrum that the discipline of theology poses, some have even spoken of a "theological theology," a theological enterprise directed, shaped, and formed by a faith affirmation of the very subject matter it intends to study. This designation is the title of an article by Michael Allen in the November 2020 issue of *First Things*. In it Allen discusses how "John Webster . . . challenged the often human-centered methods that dominate a great deal of modern theology."[29] In addition some Catholics have begun speaking of Christian "integralism," which considers the submergence of everything in society under the "church" as an ecclesiastical institution. It is worth noting here again the confusion of the term "church" with the idea of religion and Christian faith. Nevertheless integralism points toward a society that is one and whole (integral) in the deepest sense of the word, i.e., a Christian culture. This push for wholeness of conception has been mounting in response to the marginalized view that religion is just a slice of the pie, and maybe even not a very important one.

I myself prefer to say that the science of theology can only function properly by being first shaped and formed by faith, then by worldview, and subsequently by Christian philosophy. Those who say "no" to that still end up not very consciously taking up elements of the current and dominant philosophies. For example, despite Karl Barth's abhorrence of natural theology and Christian philosophy, he unselfconsciously uses the existentialist philosophy of "encounter" in his "I-Thou" theology; thank you Mr. Heidegger. In fact the confusion that theology as such, because of its subject matter, inherently guarantees right formation and integration has

28. Calvin, *Institutes*, 1.6.1–2.
29. Allen, "Theological Theology," 19–23.

blinded many to the desperate, secularized state of theology in the modern, post-Enlightenment period. My own experience in college, seminary, and graduate school in religious studies has been that theology has become one of the most secular disciplines in the academy. It creates more confusion with regard to its subject matter than genuine insight.

I would say at this point in my introduction that this state of confusion in the discipline is one of the reasons I left theology behind. It is also the reason for my deliberate decision not to use the term "theology" in the title of this book. Naturally religion and sacred texts can be studied, as can the church, and Christian teachings, and the creeds throughout the Christian era. But the confusion inherent in the term "theology" is a good reason to diminish its use dramatically. Furthermore, I would ask whether there is not a potentially blasphemous attitude that the term "theology" conjures up, namely that God can be an object of study or the object of a science. In my view, that prevailing attitude clinches the deal against frequent use of the term when contemplating Christian perspective on this or that area of life.

CHAPTER 2

Creation and the Necessity of Christian Philosophy

THUS FAR WE HAVE noticed that Christians vindicating their intellectual responsibilities face several indispensable requirements. We shall begin by reviewing them below, bearing in mind that historically rarely has any one of them been fulfilled at the same time as all of the others. When some of these requirements and demands are neglected, the proper perception and development of the others is also jeopardized.

A. BIBLIOCENTRISM

The first requirement that should be noticed within a Reformed view of the Christian's intellectual responsibilities is that the Christian's view of things must be a total revelational view. Of course, this requirement can be misunderstood. I would say, therefore, that I have in mind here nothing other than the view that Scripture—the Christian's only source of direct revelational address—must be its own interpreter. Nothing outside of that revelation can be allowed to shape and form its message. Rather the very mind of God that is most preeminently present in it must shape the very categories by means of which that message is made concrete. The interpretation must be so immediate, so direct, and so appropriate, spiritually speaking, as to warrant the judgment that the interpretation belongs to the revelation, in the sense that it wholly comports with it and serves progressively to vindicate it.

We shall see and hear again below that, of course, the revelational content of Scripture subsequently requires a categorical expression that depends upon philosophy. Yet we have disqualified the assumption that this recourse to philosophy is inconsistent with the total sovereignty of the Word in Scripture, because philosophy can create laws and rules and categories that are shaped by and, therefore, comport with the revelational content of the Word in Scripture. We recognize the Reformation's *sui ipsius interpres* ("Scripture is its own interpreter"), and we applaud the Christian's philosophical task at one and the same time.

B. THE TWO-FOLDNESS OF REVELATION: CALVIN

A second requirement or demand that we cannot ignore is that the content of revelation must be seen to include two-foldness, namely the two-foldness of the Elder and the Younger Testaments, as well as that of creation and restoration. Creation too is part of the content of revelation and in a real sense it is nonsalvational. I refer again to the lengthy citation from Calvin that has appeared earlier in our discussion. A clear sign of Calvin's attention to the doubleness of revelation is his much-neglected placement of priority on Scripture.

Calvin's view of creation remains strongly and deliberately theocentric rather than Christocentric. Christ's "mediatorship" in creation is never viewed as "salvational" but always as "modeling" and relationally expressing the will of the Father, according to Calvin. Jesus Christ is the *second* Adam; the *morphe* or form of Christ is the form of Adam in the original creation story and represents Christ's "modeling" role. God relates to Adam in Christ as Christ in creation has a revealing, modeling, sustaining, and thus secondary role to play to *express* the Father. In creation the Son expresses the Father's word and will. Thus creation is primarily a work of the Father, and in creation the Son has a role, indeed, but only a subordinate and secondary role. The Son is "begotten" of the Father, not vice versa. This classical Trinitarian view has been called *perichoresis*.

The same doubleness of conception referred to above is present in the idea that the Bible reveals not only acts of God but also how those acts were received by human beings. To Scripture itself belong both the divine activity and human being's faith centered appropriation of that activity in the life world. The work of God recorded in Scripture immediately created the very proper means by which it was received by human beings.

To the Reformed Christian, therefore, Scripture not only witnesses to the Word of God but is the Word of God. Just because it is creational does not either make it incapable of bearing the Word or diminish its status in any way. There is no need to drive a wedge between the Word from on high and an interpretation of that Word as present in the lives of those who immediately experienced it. The fact of revelation from on high and the response of humans from below always belong together, and both are part of the same covenant history.

Another way of saying the same thing is that Scripture contains a Word spoken to listening humans, just as the preacher today speaks the Word to us in the preaching situation. The Word itself is, therefore, not just a sheer, disembodied and unoccasioned announcement or encounter. It is not just proclamation or kerygma. Rather Scripture preaches and Scripture hears; Scripture presents God and Scripture shows us how we must receive him. The Bible has its own audience, composed of people such as we are. How this audience receives the Word cannot be separated from the Word itself. The doubleness of Torah (the Elder Testament) and good news (the Younger Testament) belongs to the very heart of the Reformation's view of Scripture.

C. CREATION AS STORY AND CREATION AS THE REAL WORLD

This point leads us smoothly into another important third requirement that comprises an indispensable ingredient in my argument. Creation, the situation of human beings living out their lives in the real world, is indeed part of the revelational content of Scripture. But it is also the real world in which we live today. Where Scripture is acknowledged as the Word of God, it must also at one and the same time be granted a place in the hearer's own life. Though the Bible has its own hearers within itself, they are, after all, men and women such as we are. To accept the Bible as Word of God is to identify ourselves with the Bible's own audience. Creation is both in the Word and present outside of Scripture as the real world in which we live.

This secondary doubleness of creation itself and the revelation concerning creation means that the study of creation in scholarship includes thinking about what's in the Bible, naturally now in terms of the two-foldness of creation and restoration, and also—and this is the all-important point—of thinking biblically about "the everything else that is." Creation is both a scriptural story/teaching and the real life in which we now live. And

Scripture is given exactly with a view to our acting properly in *and thinking biblically about* "the everything else that is."

Biblically speaking, we might say that the Scriptures are not finally what we see but the light by which we see, a simile Calvin has presented in the large citation above. Several implications flow from how we are to understand the proper relation of the revelation about creation in Scripture and the revelation in creation itself.

First, it is beyond doubt for Calvin that Scripture and creation are correlative. To employ the one without the other is illegitimate. Such abstraction or isolation can only lead to a distortion of both the one exclusively used and the one erroneously eclipsed from the discussion. What we call "general revelation," or the "book of nature," is not one source of the knowledge of God and Scripture another, clearer one. "General revelation" is not knowledge of God and creation that we are capable of outside of and prior to Scripture. Rather, "general revelation" is the work of God in creation as we sinners are vaguely aware of it and actually in touch with it. And this awareness, this *sensus*, must be transformed into true and specific knowledge, i.e., into *cognitio*, to reiterate the exact language of Calvin. There is only one revelation, and there is no revelation at all for us apart from creation and Scripture as taken together in their bipolar impact. We do not have here "two books of revelation."

So also the revelation about creation in Scripture becomes mangled when isolated from the proper function it was intended to perform, namely to shed light upon life in this world, or to focus our sight upon the revelation in creation through its lens. Sin does not cut us off from the revelation of God in creation. Sin does not separate us from the structural realities of this world. Accordingly, the revelation of creation in Scripture cannot be separated from the revelation in creation itself. Scripture cannot be forced to become for us a new and independent source of a world of facts and realities, a danger admittedly present in Henry Morris's Creation Science point of view. We have not on account of sin and evil ceased to stand in touch with the world of facts which came into being when God created the world and determined its uniform patterns. We must conceive the "decrease" that sin introduces differently, for Scripture is, according to Calvin's image, the proffering not of a new world of objects but a new *perspective* on the real world that was at our disposal from the beginning.

A further point here is in effect a restatement of the first one made earlier about Calvin's metaphor, but now more in reference to the simile itself.

Creation and the Necessity of Christian Philosophy

Scripture is "spectacles" according to Calvin, and spectacles or glasses are what we see through. Glasses are used to focus our vision on a reality that surrounds us. The purpose of having a pair of glasses is the improvement of vision. The object of sight is what concerns the owner of a pair of spectacles. Surely the person does not preoccupy himself or herself with the glasses themselves, say cleaning them and cherishing them as a possession that has a significance in and of itself. Glasses are put on so that the seer can finally visually grasp the reality that is the primary object of his/her interest and concern. Glasses are only a medium in the attainment of that goal.

Accordingly, Scripture directs us away from itself to the reality of what has been given and on which it sheds light. The role of Scripture is to be a light unto our path. Analogously, as my friend Lester De Koster put it frequently, for Calvin preaching Scripture is "light for the city" (also the title of one of De Koster's books on Calvin). Allow me then to raise an important hermeneutical question that attends this understanding of Scripture as dependent on Calvin's simile.

If Scripture is the light by which we see, we must attend to and have at our disposal more than the text of the Bible. The Bible is primarily light revelation, light for life, not fact revelation. This means that we are expected to acquaint ourselves with the world as we read Scripture exactly for the purpose of reading it rightly, or exactly for the purpose of reading it as it was intended to be read and used. Without familiarity with the world and extra-biblical materials, the Bible itself is provided with no application in the broadest sense and is consequently prevented even from being interpreted. "General" and "special" revelation are correlative and this means that if that to which the Bible is directed, that to which it applies, is eclipsed from the discussion, the Bible becomes misused.

It is appropriate here to mention again the view of Henry Morris, the founder of the Creation Research Society. For him much in Scripture and much of what we take from the text is used to fulfill the role of fact gathering about creation reality, an activity that is normally the task of the scientific enterprise. We might also add the similar[1] mistake of taking a few common words of Jesus, as given, e.g., in the Sermon on the Mount, and turning them into political policies without doing or having done the hard work of political analysis to determine what constitutes equitable support. We need the light by which we need to see *plus* a study of the object matter

---

1. Morris, *World Is Made of Glass*.

of political realities to come to a proper integration of faith and learning and to come to a proper use of Jesus' parabolic words.

The upshot at this point is that the Bible is not a substitute for reflection. The Bible is not a stock of facts that receive application when we repeat or reconstruct them in our contemporary efforts to live as Christians in this world. The Bible is not an alternative to the pursuance of those normal processes of thought and action that compose our life in this world. On the contrary, the only proper place that Scripture can demand is that of being allowed to regulate, direct, and norm the processes of reflection and action in which every Christian must engage to live meaningfully as God intends us to in this world.

Therefore, on the basis of Scripture itself, on the basis of its never absent reference to creation and to the lives of those who received the direct divine address, it should be said that embarrassment about the use of extra- and nonbiblical materials in the effort to determine what God expects of us is unwarranted. The law-Word of God is written (Torah), but it is also the Tao of the creation in which we live. *Torah and Tao belong together*. Indeed, Scripture should inspire the use of such materials from creational realities even to the extent of providing a concrete interpretative framework or structure of concreteness in which Scripture's own belief content is lent a definite sense. If indeed general and special revelation correlate, then we should not hesitate to employ our understanding and its results in the clarification of what Scripture requires of us. Or, even more strongly, we should experience as a requirement the task of "reading into the Bible" what sanctified reason discovers in its reflection upon the creation. There is no conflict between God's revelation in creation, our Christian discernment of it, and the revelation once-for-all delivered to us in Scripture. Not to conceive the use of Scripture in such a manner is to impute to the Christian faith an understanding of revelation that it has never historically possessed. To turn a misguided admiration of the Bible into a standard of orthodoxy is at best a misunderstanding and at its worst can lead to biblicistic aberrancy.

D. THEOLOGY NEEDS CHRISTIAN PHILOSOPHY

A fourth requirement that we have argued against in the prevailing trends in secular philosophy as well as in much theology is this: if theology is reflection on the content of biblical revelation as well as how that content is interpreted by the church, then it seems evident that theology needs

Creation and the Necessity of Christian Philosophy

Christian philosophy. In fact all theologies continue to use philosophy, whether that is acknowledged or not. Once again, I would ask, from where does the theme of the "I-Thou encounter" come in much twentieth-century theology, for example as it is found in the theology of Karl Barth? Thank you again, Mr. Heidegger.

One might appropriately call this unacknowledged conflation the "New Modernism." Indeed, philosophy is not, systemically speaking, an unbelieving alternative to theology. The two, philosophy and theology, perform different and supplementary functions. Without Christian philosophy, thinking about the content of revelation hangs in midair and goes nowhere. Without Christian philosophy, continuing reflection on the content of revelation becomes disembodied rhetoric and thin soup preaching that is quickly forgotten. Moreover, disembodied rhetoric is easily susceptible of ideological distortion, exploitation, and misuse. Where there is no Christian philosophy, other secular philosophies take up the space one way or another.

I wish to make a major point here that the content of revelation in Scripture is nothing in itself. It can hover in midair over the reality about which concern is being expressed. And, finally, worst of all, it can acquire its meaningfulness as a mirror for the prevailing historical or cultural ethos. Consider this example. In the 1970s part of the content of Christian revelation along with its application was adapted to Marxist analysis. This hybrid concord came to be called "liberation theology." It became an egregious example of what happens to the revelational content of Scripture when the task of philosophizing in the Christian community of faith is ignored while at the same time the demand for concreteness and application remains urgent. This happens too when the Christ message of the Younger Testament is left dangling in thin air and separated from the Elder word of the Hebraic worldview of Yeshua of Nazareth ("Jesus" in the Greek language).

E. CHRISTIAN PHILOSOPHY IS REAL AND LEGITIMATE

We must move on to a discussion of a fifth requirement that has emerged in the argument thus far. It is that philosophy that is legitimate and helpful for theology is genuinely philosophy even if it has a profound connection with revelation. It need be no embarrassment to a philosopher to have experienced a Christian faith formation or to have experienced that that connection outfits the philosopher with certain beliefs that control the weighing and designing of theories in a discipline. Such an attachment to revelation does not make the philosophy in question theology or less than good philosophy.

We can make this claim because we realize that all knowledge is personal and analogical, that it arises from a movement of the heart, and that therefore there is no "pure philosophy." As David Bentley Hart once said, "the unyielding rationalist turns out to be the most irrational fideist of all: one who believes in reason even though there cannot possibly be a reason for that belief."[2]

Furthermore, since there is more than one way to connect with subjectivity, philosophy is not a preoccupation and a value possessed only by those who reflect upon the everything that is apart from biblical revelation. Of course, we know by this point in the argument that philosophy such as is being discussed here is not about the Bible. We can insist without embarrassment and apology, nevertheless, that Scripture has a role in philosophy. Such philosophy is engaged in vindicating the Word without scandalizing philosophy and the philosophical task. There is nothing incompatible about *sola Scriptura* and the philosophical task.

F. THE NECESSITY OF CHRISTIAN PHILOSOPHY

We are now prepared for a deduction of the final requirement, because all of the ingredients necessary to warrant my concluding claim are present. Before stating it, I simply ask the reader to keep clearly in mind my plea for doubleness of conception at many levels. I have spoken of the doubleness of the Elder and Younger Testaments, of creation and restoration, of the revelation of creation in Scripture and of the life world of creation itself, of Scripture and biblical vision or worldview, and finally of the philosophical and theological tasks. Only a willingness to accept the cognitive complexity of these matters can have taken us this far without falling into the trap of playing off one term over against another.

We have rejected the argument that philosophy is necessarily an unbelieving alternative to theology. But we also reject the more traditional arrangement and conventional alignment of philosophy and theology on the model of nature and grace, a view that dominated the Catholic tradition and has shaped a lingering Scholastic influence in Protestantism. Therefore, we are invited to accept that there is an intimate and intrinsic relation

2. Hart, "Reason's Faith."

between biblical revelation and the task of philosophizing that takes place within the Christian community. In other words, we can navigate safely past the Scylla and Charybdis of revealed versus natural knowledge, or revelation and reason, or theology and philosophy, by affirming the project of Christian philosophy. *This will help in minimizing the historical misuse of the term "theology" as a misleading stand-in for "Christian perspective."* Not all Christian persons using Christian perspective in their thinking are theologians.

Creation is a real part of the essential two-fold content of revelation, and understanding this cuts off at the root the notion of "nature" or "being-in-itself." *Creation* is not just a revelational element of the biblical content but the real world in which we all live, and this makes the project of Christian philosophizing conceivable. The advantages that we gain by this affirmation are many. If one considers the long logic of mistakes that typifies the history of the doctrine of creation and of the epistemological problems that have attended it, a new avenue of progress is opened. For example, safely within the Reformed Christian tradition the opportunity is given to transcend that far too familiar Christian arrangement and rearrangement of the content of revelation that goes nowhere and finally even becomes susceptible of current cultural distortion.

In addition, we also have the opportunity to escape Christian revelational or Christocratic speculation, a pressure that has been applied to the content of biblical revelation when philosophy is spurned as unbelief and when the content of revelation is reduced to what is purely gracious and Christic.

Finally, and most crucially, we can be set free from the invasion by and overwhelming of the revelational content of Christianity by secular concepts and structures that Christian philosophy has not itself produced from within itself. It is from these mistakes, continuing throughout the centuries without much noticeable variation, that we can be liberated and given the freedom to create a new awareness that is both thoroughly biblical and firmly attached to this world.[3]

---

3. See Paul Tyson's interesting discussion of the necessity of a "Christian metaphysics of nature and a Christian epistemology" in his recent book *A Christian Theology of Science*. "No matter," he says, that such an enterprise will get "no oxygen in the public, secular sphere" because "there are still large-enough Christian communities and Christian knowledge institutions for Christians to start rolling in their own spaces." *Christian Theology of Science*, 180–81. See also his prefaces to this conclusion. *Christian Theology of Science*, 169–76.

My conclusion that Christian philosophy is affirmable and necessary could not have been reached without beginning our reflection with the theme of *creation*. We have had to investigate creation faith's gradual diminishment and final eclipse (more about that later) and the reasons that brought it about. And we have had to unravel, therefore, a complicated logic of errors, which mistakes have continued with some variations and with significant consequences throughout the Christian centuries. They have accumulated in a buildup of varying arguments against the necessity of Christian philosophy. A believing view of *creation* brings this tragic misunderstanding to an end.

CHAPTER 3

Mystery, the Limits of Knowledge, and Our Approach to Scripture

A. MYSTERY

As we approach the topic of creation as the story appears in Scripture, it is appropriate to comment on the preliminary matter of *mystery*. There is the ineffable and the incomprehensible. God is a mystery, a tremendous mystery, as Rudolph Otto once put it. He is essentially incomprehensible, as Calvin argues in the first chapters of book 1 of the *Institutes*. For God to be known, he must tell us about himself. Nicholas of Cusa wrote extensively about human limits, calling his view "the doctrine of learned ignorance."[1] I would not have said this when I was twenty-five, or thirty-five, or even forty-five. But as one passes by the "three score years and ten," one comes to the feeling of absolute dependence more frankly and openly.

Not only is God the fundamental mystery, but the cosmos is fundamentally mysterious as well. We do not naturally know the why and wherefore of things present and forevermore. Do things have a beginning? If so, where do they come from? What was the beginning like? And why is there a cosmos rather than not one?

What about the great conundrum of evil? Does evil belong to the nature of things? Is it simply a part of the system? Or is it a surd factor, a foreign element, introduced into life by the bad choices of God's creatures?

---

1. Cusanus, *Of Learned Ignorance*.

This is a huge uncertainty. The same applies to human life. Why are we here? What is life all about? Where did we come from and whence do we go? And finally, to round it all out, what is death, and is there anything beyond it? Death is one of the darkest mysteries of all.

Noticing these matters and making mention of them is not a way of dodging questions. That is often the accusation made when one references "mystery," as if it were a way of avoiding issues or giving up on developing difficult answers. However, the intention in this present discussion is to plead the case that we are not using an escape hatch, but that at last we are ready to face reality. As we ourselves age, we see more clearly that it is not given to the mind to grasp everything, to figure matters out naturally, though all peoples and all persons try, each in their own way, communally and individually. We all try to make as much sense of things as we can. Even "science" has become a barricade behind which many hide their fears and avoidance of the unknown. So we create our stories, our explanations, and our "answers" to the riddles of life.

As is clear by now, I follow Calvin in saying that the answers are unknowable relying on our own energies and resources. Relying on ourselves we come up with myriad answers, many of which will conflict with one another among the peoples of the world, past and present. Calvin's own view is even stronger. Invariably our own stories, our own identification of the only comforts in life and in death, become idolatrous. Invariably we seek a key to the solution of the whole within life, in some thing or person or interest that is not made to bear the load that only the transcendent and incomprehensible God is able to do. We cannot produce the story ourselves. It can only be given by a God who is in charge of the knowledge of himself and thus also in charge of the knowledge of us, since the two are intimately related.

It is with this great not-knowing that we must face the question of the origin of all things. If we believe that there is someone beyond the origin, we can have some sense of a beginning in the absolute sense. If there is no origin (as natural reason suggests it), if everything is an eternal principle, even if only a meager quantum of dust and energy, a speck from which it all exploded, or just maybe even the law of gravity, then there need be no one prior to and radically outside of the everything that is.

The biblical way that the conundrum of existence is addressed is with the creation story of Genesis. And the Genesis approach is essentially an assertion that what our most distant human predecessors and authors of the creation text of the Bible had and knew *experientially* was essentially the beginning, *for whatever anyone can ever know.*

B. THE LIMITS OF KNOWLEDGE

As I approach the Genesis texts relating to creation, I must reiterate that I approach the issues of Christian thought with a philosophical bent. I have always been inclined to think about life as a whole and then first and foremost in terms of its relationship to God. I still believe that approach takes precedence over theology, even informing theology and shaping it, as it should any other discipline or science.

From the previous section of this chapter and its discussion of mystery, I have also more recently become much more aware of the limits of knowledge, of all knowledge. Life is a mystery and the world we inhabit so overwhelming and so infinite in extent and significance that we can only hope to skim the surface. Also, we stand at one point in the process of creation's development and history, with all the attendant limitations that entails. All of our current thinking is culturally relative, and we should always remind ourselves of that fact. Moreover, we cannot grasp and control it with our minds. In fact we need to surrender our minds to it. It is not clear that theology does that, or knows how to do it, as is the case with many of the disciplines.

I have always viewed God as a supreme being, as our Father essentially. He is the one on whom we are absolutely dependent in all things. We all have some basic sense of God, that there is someone who is in control of all of life and the universe that we inhabit. I experience God strongly as "our Father in heaven." Indeed, God shows himself to be more than our Creator and sustainer. In a very broken world he also has an ultimately merciful, i.e., Christic, countenance. And, in addition, he is always with us in Spirit and in truth (faithful to his character). He makes himself known to us in mysterious ways.

Is this classic Christian trinitarianism? I do not think so. That idea has been developed by theology into an elaborate doctrine about which tomes have been written, as if it can be figured out. Significant to my experience is the fact, as we turn to Scripture, that this idea is *not* taught in the Bible. Indeed God is referred to now as Father, then as Son, and then again as Holy Spirit in many places in Scripture. He is indeed described in tripartite terms. I do not understand this mystery. My reaction is, leave it alone.

This doctrine of the Trinity is indeed exactly that, i.e., an idea developed over time in the early history of the Christian church. As a doctrine, it goes significantly beyond Scripture. "Three persons in one essence" is not an idea present in the Bible, especially as one turns to the Greek ideas and terms used. It is actually an idea developed in strong dependence on the dominant intellectual culture of Greco-Roman antiquity. However, it also had another important motivation, as J. N. D. Kelly points out so well. This new teaching was seized upon in order to set out as clearly as possible the Christian view of God in contrast to the aberrant views that began to emerge after the Younger Testament period.[2] The same applies to how it was that the early church began to define the coexistence of the human and the divine in Jesus Christ. None of us could have done better, were we faced with the challenges of the early church.

We do not live in the first two or three centuries after the Younger Testament period. We live some two thousand years later. We are not obligated to defend and develop these doctrines in the way in which they were in the early church. Who are we anyway to say who and what God is, to write thousands of pages about his "essence," his inner life, and his being? Or even worse, who are we to say what he was planning to do "before" he created the cosmos? I wonder at times if he may be laughing about all of these efforts to explain who he is and what he was or is thinking.

Existentially our efforts at explanation will not get us beyond our questions. As I have argued in the previous section, we all must face our mortality and the apparent unfairness that the major consequence of life is the cruelty of death. Theology is not our only comfort in life and in death. Actually, far from it. This is especially so since much modern academic theology is saturated with skepticism and suspicion. It is consummately the science of the "yes-but."

Faith, I think, begins with God, the God who put into place all of this that we call life. It is of little use to start theologizing about this God and who he is in himself and his "attributes." We do not know. It is as simple as that. As Calvin put it, we have a vague creaturely awareness of the presence of a higher power or supreme being. We sense that we are under him and ultimately dependent on him in all things. We have a deeply seated recognition or *sensus* of a God, and we have ongoing responses to God's order in creation. Calvin did not *start with God*. In this sense he was a thinker

---

2. Kelly, *Early Christian Creeds*.

radically different from many others. Calvin begins with the *knowledge* of God and of ourselves.

We can go on and on trying on our own to make sense of this experience. Inevitably we will each go in many different directions if we do not simply leave it to God to tell us about himself. The story of the religions of the world is the story of humans trying their best to assuage the not-knowing, the mystery, and the anxiety of it by drawing on their own resources and imaginations. Humans cannot endure the mystery without persisting in their efforts to explain it to themselves. Hence the origin of the religions of the world.

None of this vague apprehension (*sensus*) counts as "right knowledge" or *cognitio* until informed by the revelation of God in Scripture, to paraphrase Calvin. In fact without Scripture these givens immediately turn into the misappropriation of this or that intramundane person, or thing, or interest as the key to the solution of the whole. Calvin goes so far as to say that under those circumstances we even lose the "image of God," i.e., true knowledge, righteousness, and holiness.[3]

The worldwide scene of unending human imaginings of the various religious groups is bizarre, to say the least. In some ways it is, of course, instructive, giving all of us a good sense of "holy envy," to use the insightful phrase of Barbara Brown Taylor. Listen to the ancient religion of the Zoroastrian Gnostics; the mythologies of the Egyptians and ancient Greeks; the more literal humanizations of God among the Greek philosophers; the Gnostic myths that besieged and tempted both Jews and Christians; the multitude of ancient Asian and Oriental representations; the Inca and Aztec gods; the amazing ruminations and rituals of Native Americans; the truly astonishing nature religions of the Africans; the endless emergence of quasi-Christian cults of all forms, especially in the US, from Christian Science to Mormonism and the rest. We could go on and on. Human beings everywhere and at all times are desperately trying to figure out who God is, what he is doing, and how we figure into the picture.

There is so much we cannot know for sure. Uniquely Calvin says that even to begin to figure out this God whose presence we sense, we need his direct help from the outset. Even for a knowledge of his existence and of his role in bringing all existents into being, we stand in need of him and his direction. In short, we need his "memoirs" and sagas about it all. He must tell us what is the case about this fundamental matter. And so quite consistently

---

3. Calvin, *Commentaries on Genesis*, 139.

in this "memoir" God turns us to his *works*, about which we must read in *the text* to comprehend his *identity*. He is after all *who he will be*.[4]

C. OUR APPROACH TO SCRIPTURE: BELIEVING IN IT FIRST

I continue to give Scripture a special place in the conundrum of life. In addition there is the grueling, puzzling, mysterious matter of the brokenness of all things. Are good and evil coterminous? Have they always existed side by side? Or is God essentially innocent? We need God's help to approach these difficult questions, and in this capacity, they are addressed in Scripture. Either we receive the basic story about God, about ourselves, and about the "theatre of the divine glory"[5] from God, or we have to create it on our own. We all want to know, even though we do not have the natural capacity to figure it out.

It is important to notice that the beginning of the biblical saga is a narrative, an autobiography. It is important to emphasize that here even though undoubtedly the Genesis story was composed from the retrospective glance of a much later situation. There were no humans on site when God created the world. No one, no matter what the capacity or stance, is able to get back to the origin to observe it directly. By "no one" we also must include today's vaunted "scientists." In fact in the very character of the story we are told that the origin is unreachable by humans, either by or through faith reflection or by the tools and instruments of rule-governed thought that we call "science."

The narrative of origins in the Bible is written from the retrospective glance of an already quite developed and completed creation order since no one other than God was there to observe his first movement outside of himself. Thus the saga is "from" and "about" the human author's primary experience of the life world. It is fitting to refer to the story as a "saga" or "narrative" because the Bible does not contain so-called scientific facts. However, that does not mean that the Bible, also in Genesis, does not speak correctly or that it does not speak the Truth. At the very beginning of Scripture the measure and source of that is the *human* author's common sense and everyday "pre-scientific" experience.

---

4. Exod 3:14. The Hebrew verb is in the future tense.
5. Calvin, *Institutes* 1.51.

Mystery, the Limits of Knowledge, and Our Approach to Scripture

Many have observed that the situation of the origin of the narrative evidences minimally a commonsense, agrarian context. This comports with the reality that the texts of Genesis in the Bible are likely not themselves the oldest texts of the Elder Testament. Although the texts in question speak about the oldest "events" of the universe, more than likely they are not themselves the oldest texts. The human author is speaking out of a situation very different than the situation of the origin itself that remains shrouded in an unfathomable and divine "*mysterium tremendum*."

These facts alone tell us that the *origin is unreachable in an absolute sense* and that therefore we must be satisfied with the account that has been bequeathed to us by God himself through the agency of human authors living in ancient Israel. The author Moses in turn is essentially describing the world in which he lives. The author is implying that his life world with its roughly given differences of things is what we have received from the hand of God in the beginning *for all anyone can ever know*.

"For all anyone can ever know" is the decisive concept here. It is decisive for the ordinary human being and thus decisive for all human beings, no matter what tools they try to use. Either we begin with this God validated saga and its truth claims, which must not be mistaken for so-called scientific facts, or we construct one of our own, by ourselves, without the help of the Creator. We all live by story when it comes to the basic questions of life: believer, unbeliever, anti-believer, or believer in an alternate story. We are all in the same epistemic situation. And this predicament includes all human beings. It also includes those who engage in the rarefied and abstractive activity of historical and language critical science, or second order, rule-governed and abstractive thought. Paul Tyson in his *A Christian Theology of Science* says it well: "Our facts are always mythically framed."[6]

We can accept the story as a basic belief, or we can pretend to go after the putative "facts"[7] on our own, alleging that we are in no way dependent on a basic story because we have set such matters aside procedurally and intentionally. Much modern science in fact pretends that just such an approach is possible, an approach that is essentially free of pre- and nonscientific basic beliefs. Those who take up these approaches falsely privilege themselves with a stance that assumes they can trace the process of the coming into being of things without the introduction of paradigms, models, hunches, and extrapolations.

6. Tyson, *Christian Theology of Science*, 143.
7. Hudson, *Cult of the Fact*.

After years of study of creation thought, I remain convinced that science is subject to the same limits of knowledge that all human beings are subject to in the ordinary situation of givenness. I am also convinced that much of the scientific pursuit of the mystery of origins is a not so subtly concealed attempt to trace the steps in the process of the origination of the universe with *human* tools alone so that no God need be introduced in order for it all to make sense.

The quasi-religious drive behind the exertions of much science today reminds me of the common pursuit among many to fantasize about the existence of life on other planets, or in other distant places in the universe. The biblical view claims geocentricity *in the religious (not astronomical) sense*. "In the beginning God created the heavens and the earth. And *the earth* was unformed and void." This may stick in the craw of secular scientists and motivate them to seek signs of life elsewhere in the universe in order to test or diminish the biblical narrative's perspective or put it on the defensive. The Catholic Church was not entirely wrong when it first questioned the motives behind Galileo's claims.

What picture does the Genesis story bequeath us about the universe and its essential nature? Even as we fully realize that it is not on-site reporting, we can recognize it as a religious saga that attempts to state the meaning and significance of things at their foundation. The text is not the product of rule-governed thought. It is not science. But nonetheless, even a saga, a story, a narrative, or a myth can put forward truth claims. For example, who of us has not read works of fiction and discovered in them important and truthful things about life?

Even if not science, Scripture's creation narrative may nonetheless have something important to say. It merits our careful thought. There are beliefs in the text that may indeed be able to function in science as beliefs that do control, or can control, the designing of theories. To say that the biblical text is not science is not to say that there is nothing in the text that might be relevant for the doing of science.

Scientific efforts to explain are also in fact controlled by what there is in the mind of the scientist pre-theoretically, originally, and natively. One might accept as direct observation what the naturalist does observing bird calls in the wild and distinguishing the calls of one species from another. The observer is significant in this activity. The observer provides the ears or the recorder. Slightly different but consistent with the same notion of observation is the scientist who conducts an experiment by setting up limiting conditions for the sake of focus and then triggers an event that is observed as it occurs. This for example might be what happens when a chemist puts the flame of a Bunsen burner under a test tube to observe at what temperature a substance changes from solid to liquid. These are simple examples, but they are sufficient to remind us that the scientific method is based on the intention of the scientist to make an observation. Implicit in the use of the scientific method is the establishment of stated conditions, the purpose of which is to focus on a particular reality, and then to use direct observation to give some accounting of that reality.

Sometimes the observation is direct, but at other times it is accomplished by collecting data recorded at many different times and possibly by many different observers using a wide variety of tools. Consider, for example, the prevalence today of "modeling." Time can limit the exercise of the scientist's methods. In the case of past events, they are no longer directly observable. Some sequelae may still be observable, but the original event that triggered a sequence of events is past, and in that sense, it is out of our reach for direct observation. In an effort to explore that earlier event scientists create models beginning with some current observation and extrapolate what might have (although usually the implication is that it *must* have) happened previously in such a way that it could have led to what is now still in the range of our observation. Of course this leaves a gap in the theory, because concluding what might have been does not ensure that it is what was. Models are guesses. In dealing with history or past events scientists depend on models.

The limitation of models is based on two factors. First, that the proportion of actual collectable data between the event now witnessed and the previous condition we are trying to explain or account for is disproportionate. So, for example, a model may be used to explain the relationship between a present event that is observable and something that happened millions of years ago. In between the present and the long past event there is a nearly inestimable quantity of data that the scientist must skip through from point to point to explain the connection between the two. What remains to be considered is the proportion of other possible and even relevant events that we choose to ignore so that we may move to our conclusion. This massive quantity of unobserved and unexplained events we simply wrap up into a model, a metaphor of sorts to explain that on which we are choosing to focus.

The second limit that is often neglected is the possibility that as soon as we step into the use of models, with their inevitable mass of missing information, we have before us the opportunity for using many alternative models, each of which might be used to explain the same thing. When we are impressed by the function of our model, we may be tempted to use it to explain far more than it really can. In the process the model may take on a life of its own and become an argument rather than a tool. If we are convinced by our own model, we are inclined to accept as fact the missing pieces that we ourselves have filled in. For example, many visitors to museums of natural history may wonder how one bone and some plastic turn into a dinosaur. On a more juvenile level we might think of the dot-to-dot figures children create by following the numbers from one dot to the next until a figure emerges that they can recognize.

This limitation of models tended to make scientists cautious about their use in the past, but the development of computer technology and the possibility of processing huge quantities of disparate data has made us much bolder in assembling models. The question of course still remains: What have we chosen to ignore and what are the missing pieces?

Now back to the text of Scripture to see if there might be something there that is of use in our thinking as well as in the doing of science. Surely the biblical text claims that there is a God. It makes that assumption unequivocally. Moreover, the *believer* takes that claim to be indeed a fact, even when there are so many who say the text is myth and mean by that "not fact." The text also claims that there is an absolute origin. It puts this forth as a fact, not a speculation or a possibility. Those who believe the text are thus equipped with two claims that they regard as being the case, two claims that transcend the distinction between "how" and "why" with which so-called theistic evolutionists begin their endeavors. The two claims of the believer are not science, but for sure they are relevant for the doing of science.

In addition and even as important is the idea that the world as we experience it and the world as the author of the text experienced it, with its many different entities and kinds, is the world as we received it in the beginning from the hand of God, *at least for all we can know*. Creation is beyond the limits of all thought, and therefore we need the author, of both the creation and of the text about it, to tell us. It is worth considering whether the desire to trace or model or explain God's steps and methods might be off limits.

Mystery, the Limits of Knowledge, and Our Approach to Scripture

We must therefore begin with the world of our ordinary experience, or, more specifically, the world of the experience of the text's author, who, like us, lived in an already quite complete creation. That creation in which the author found himself surely housed a diversity of entities and things, each ordered and described according to its kind (in the ordinary experiential sense), or genus, or kingdom to which it belonged. In fact the author uses the device of the seven-day week to arrange this variety in an ascending order of complexity, from the simplest elements of light, air, earth, sun, moon, stars, on to planets, plants, living creatures, and finally on to human beings themselves. Each is assumed to have been created according to its kind and appears in a specific order onto the scene of creation.

As we move forward here, we will repeatedly come back to this basic assertion: on the basis of the saga's basic beliefs, none of the diversity presented there can be reduced to some one element or prior, single entity or thing. Each has an integrity of its own as it does in our ordinary, naïve experience, and this places a fundamental limit on our thinking of things and our accounting of their origin.

So we see again and again that it does no real good to separate religion and science categorically, as if the former deals just with what we believe to be the case and the latter with what we can know factually to be the case. Even Kant had overcome that quite primitive epistemology of the early Enlightenment and that of the earlier rationalist traditions. As we approach Scripture, we shall see that what we believe to be the case may indeed include what is the case. Moreover, what we describe as factually the case most often also involves beliefs, hunches, and other such premeditations. With respect to the major creation text of the Bible, it is fair to say that there is no science there, at least not on the face of it. But it does not follow from this that the text presents no data relevant information that could be useful in the proper weighing and designing of theories in the various disciplines that explore those things that exist.

I do not wish to jump ahead to the text and to other myths that may differ from it. But I do wish to suggest here already that the idea that the universe is billions and billions of years old and that the original something out of which everything subsequently evolved was simply a primordial quantum of dust and energy, or even just the law of gravity, is as much a story as the Bible's story that God called into being out of nothing the diversity described in the text according to the scheme of the seven-day week. As even many scientists acknowledge, these two stories have the same epistemic status. Both show that we can know virtually nothing about the absolute beginning of things. Both testify strongly to the limits of all human knowledge with respect to those things that existed outside the limits of any human's experience.

Before I turn to the human author of the narrative or saga, one more comment is fitting. I consider it irrelevant to scope out whether we think of one author or several. One of the clearest statements resolving this puzzling is that of C. S. Lewis, who often said about such historical critical questions that the text lies before us; let's get on with it![8] The author of the creation story was writing from out of a situation of an already developed and completed creation. The author was "projecting," and I truly mean that in the best sense of the word. Allow me to defend that claim in its most positive sense. What else could any human being have done if involved meaningfully in the telling of the story, as Moses, God's great prophet, was?

Since Fichte, Marx, and Freud loaded negative connotations onto the notion of "projection," we too easily jump to the conclusion that it is always a picture born out of many deeply subjective or base motives worthy of discrediting. I must admit, I am not inclined, as C. S. Lewis was not inclined, to comment much about the human author of the text. Authors are never as important as what is written; after all, it is the text itself that we are after. In this particular case it is important to see how human, noetic limits brought about what the author simply could not avoid saying and doing.

Moses was not there. Period. Only God was there. Moreover, God used Moses in his total human context to initiate the creation saga. This is the beginning of the story of his divine identity through the narration of his deeds, words, and works!

---

8. Lewis, *Screwtape Letters*, 120–21.

CHAPTER 4

The Projection of Moses from out of His Own Completed World

MOSES, THE AUTHOR OF the Genesis text for all we can know from the text itself, naturally lived long after the events of the primeval history about which he writes. These writings use older reports that may have drawn on still older oral traditions that had been extant for a long time. If we isolate the creation and fall stories of Gen 1–3, we may say that these memories and the narratives of the beliefs of the called-out people of Israel were handed down generation to generation. Because they are genealogical sagas, told by fathers and elders to their offspring, in the Hebrew Pentateuch they are commonly called *toledoth*.

The memory narratives address the fundamental conundrums of life: where did it all come from; how do we explain the omnipresent human experience of good and evil, blessing and suffering; and are there any remedies? Ultimately the narratives, whatever the date of their final compilations, are intended to reach back to the beginning, both of ancestors and the world order itself. These generational sagas are naturally coupled with certain worldview understandings of the nature and extent of sin and evil.

Moses compiled the *toledoth* and arranged them in a certain chronological order. His wish was to write about the acts of God *in the order in which they occurred*. Moses is a theocentrist; he is not trying to argue that the creation story is a story of saving responsiveness. The narrative is the theo-history. It is not first and foremost the history of the people of Israel, which story, content wise, follows later.

Moses was not on the scene when the first founding act of God occurred in the origination of creation. Though Moses wrote out of a broken world in need of redemption, he constrained himself first and foremost to writing as a theocentrist. His own needs were not the first thing. He had no need to portray the creation story as a salvation story just because he himself was in need of one, having been, for example, a murderer in ancient Egypt. As has been said previously, Moses was not on the scene when the first founding act of God occurred in the origination of creation. He was not there as God created the world. Yet Moses was deeply concerned to tell the whole story from God's point of view, as God was the primary character and actor.

As it continues to be even now, the product of that first divine action of origination, i.e., the cosmos, was and is there, as was the case for Moses as well as for all of humankind to see and experience. The foundation had been laid, as in the first step of building a house. It was a home in which they lived; they were in the middle of it. The cosmic scene was created first, and not just as the *occasion* for the later and up-coming salvation history of the Hebrews. The theater of the creation cannot be marginalized and minimized that way, as if there were a better or more important story still coming up.

Especially in the case of Moses it is a bit risky to consider the broken world, the *Sitz im Leben* or real-life situation of the author. To do so is to shift the focus to his subjective self and the conditions out of which he spoke and wrote. Moses was not able to return to the event of creation itself. Instead he looks back with his ancestors from their and his own present to the very beginning, and he does so in an effort to understand the present in which he and his fellows live.

Normally in a narrative we expect to be led by the object matter, or what is more commonly called "the subject matter," which are the realities and events about which the narrative is composed. That being the case we would not expect to be led by Moses' retrospective view. But here, at this juncture in the beginning of the biblical narrative, we do well to turn for a moment to the writer's own circumstances. There seems to be no alternative, no other option, since the human writer was not the omniscient and omnipresent actor behind all of what happened "in the beginning." Hence "the beginning" is portrayed much as Moses experienced his present, the world as Moses experienced it in his own *present* moment in time, except for the elements of sin and salvation.

The Projection of Moses from out of His Own Completed World

Many who have studied the text of Genesis have remarked that the story's setting is both agricultural and civilizational. The setting as the product of the divine activity is a garden, but a garden that includes a *cultural mandate*! Moreover, Moses did not write mythologically, as most of the surrounding civilizations had done. In those myths there are many gods, each representing some important piece of human experience and life. There is war and there are the gods of war; there is fertility and there are the gods of fertility; there is love and friendship and there are gods of the various attachments. But in Hebraism, in Moses' case, no pieces or dimensions of the world order are divinized; rather all that comes into being through creation is nondivinized.

There is God and there is the creation and the being of neither overlaps the other. God is the sovereign maker/ruler of all things visible and invisible. In this basic respect the *toledoth* saga of Moses and the people is set apart from the myths of their neighbors. And it is all projected by Moses out of his collective imagination onto the past, right back down to the beginning; for Moses there is an *absolute* beginning. Living as far from that beginning as Moses did, there could have been no other way than *projecting* if, he, Moses, the human writer, was to be a *real* part of narrative as its *human* author. God and creatures like Moses were always intended to be linked and thus to work together. The divine author, God, respects and accepts the writing of Moses as adequate for the expression of his written word.

When we use the term "myth," we commonly think, "Oh, that's fiction." The same commonly applies to the use of the term "projection." We say sneeringly, "Oh, he's projecting" in order to discredit an account, as if it were delusional. Yet there is nothing in principle objectionable about "projection" in this case. It may indeed reflect that Moses was at his epistemic limits when it came to telling of the creation event itself, *as all human beings still are* when operating without Moses' saga.

Projection, in this instance of Moses' narrative, is not a concept for the deconstruction of flawed characters but actually for constructions that benefit the narrative's hearers. It is part of the human constitution. It is a sign within us that we are surrounded by and grounded in something more, something above and beyond, to which we are all as human beings drawn, like metal to a magnet. Projection actually indicates that there is a God rather than no god.

There is One who draws us out of ourselves to that to which everything points. Far from indicating that there is no god, or that god is a product of our imagination, projection shows that there is the One to whom all things are drawn. Projection is a sign and sense of divinity; it is, of course, not knowledge of God, but it is the mark within us that grounds the knowledge of God and in which that ground is made concrete and specific. We by nature move toward God because God has always been moving toward us first.

It could not have happened any other way. God uses Moses in his created humanness, not outside of it. That is the first astonishing manner in which God shows how he loves what he has created. The biblical witness is not fond of magic. All peoples have done this, from many ages past. And all continue to do it in their own ways. Those ways may be surprisingly different in the present in comparison to what they were in the past, but the schema is similar.

Undoubtedly there are correspondences, comparisons, and analogies among the sagas, the various religions of mankind. This is unavoidable. All assert, intuit, sense, imagine a divine one and an origin, if there is a divine being. In the modern myth there is often no divine one because there is no real origin and thus likely no need for a divine, almighty maker of heaven and earth. All the sagas address the role of persons in this cosmos, the amazing initiative and response of the human creature in this cosmos of freedom, fascination, and the fulfillment of opportunity.

And sagas speak, each in their own collective ways, to the place and role of good and evil and its resolution in the world, or in the world to come. Creation/fall/recreation is like a universal and ineluctable "structural schema" in human existence. We might think here of Kant's schema of "god, freedom, and immortality," a fundamental and universal structure of the pure practical reason. Moreover, variations on this schema are abundant because the realities referenced were there first and continue to be there irrespective of the exactly proper human grasp of them.

We stand before Moses' projection of this whole saga, story, narrative, or *toledoth*. Moses projects all the way back into the primal narrative, and he does so from his place in his own present moment; as all peoples must do and generally have done. The world that Moses lived in and experienced is, *for all anyone can ever know*, the world that we all have received originally from the hand of God. Initially it was all also only "very good." Let me

The Projection of Moses from out of His Own Completed World

repeat, *as Gen 1 does numerous times*, that it was all originally very good, without sin and thus without the need for salvation!

Humans project because that is how the reality that has happened and is still with us comes home to us, expresses itself in our lives, comes through to us. It is the best we can do, and it is thus also the way in which the mystery breaks in upon us and into our lives. It is the way the limits of knowledge expose themselves.

Were there no beginning and thus no maker, had there been no subsequent disruption of the peace, and no real remedy to the disruption, there would be no projection, no effort to get at the meaning of the whole. But the world order is not purely fluid or mere random data. It would not keep bothering us, puzzling us, drawing us into some faith, some belief, some resolution, and some relief if there had been no "in the beginning" and no God who brought it all about. We would be blank, and there would be no "projection" at all. The cynical exposure of the definition of the term "projection" is a symptom, a sign of atheism.

The reality of God is expressed in the *persistence* of our many varied projections. The reality is the magnet, and we are the pieces of metal being drawn to that reality. Projection is no mere expression of the human subject; rather it is itself an expression of how the reality is there and how it keeps impinging on us with its cosmic force, the *force majeure* of God and the work of his hands. This applies not only to the patterned order of the cosmos (the law idea) but as well to the basic themes/schemas of our life-views themselves. The ontic reality is necessarily coupled with a corresponding and parallel epistemic one. The ontic reality is necessarily coupled with a spiritive, religious *push* in all things toward God.

Out of his situation and the situation of his ancestors, as known to him out of the *toledoth*, Moses describes the beginning and what happened in the beginning with persons and God in the original picture. Moses does this in order to express his story and the narrative of his people. There is God; there is a beginning of all things invisible and visible (the heavens and the earth). Moreover, it was all very good, truly good, good in the most fundamental sense; so good in fact that the point had to be repeated a score of times in Gen 1 to make it clear and unmistakable.

Unfortunately there is also subsequently the creature's willful transgression, and there was and is human freedom. There is as well a story of creation and fall in Gen 2:4b and the passages that follow. There is most definitely no in-built dross. Thus nothing really makes any sense without freedom, which sheds some light on the mystery of evil, though it does not explain it as fully as we might desire. Finally there is at last the call to be faithful and to be responsible earthlings in the present as well as in the final resolution in the life everlasting. Universally these are the principles of the human saga because creational experience is very good and reliable on the face of it. The experience is foundational; it is a true testimony to the basic realities of life.

In the nineteenth and twentieth centuries these experiences were considered to be ways in which human beings themselves have to create meanings and values because, in essence, the cosmos is unknowable, only a totally fluid order, and all cultural positivizations are purely subjective products. There is consciousness and its coping devices on the one hand, and there is the unreachable "thing in itself," or reality as it is in itself, on the other. In this bewildering situation humans cope, articulate their "values," create their various meanings, try to assuage their fears, and struggle to survive.

What if our projections are *not* the best we can do for creating a meaningful life in our minds and thus in our cultures? What if the projections are leading us to other realities? Can the projections not also be reliable, at least in some general sense? Kant and others like him created the modern theory of projections, but they always separated the projections from some unknowable "reality as it is in itself," some *Ding an sich*.

Creation teaches that the workings of humans and the workings of the human mind, though up against real limits, are trustworthy, do not lead us astray altogether, can indeed be a starting place. No individual or group of individuals can grasp or project the whole, everything that is and every meaning that is present. The connection is there. The very persistent acts of projection testify to the realities outside of themselves, even though we see through a glass darkly.

We see through a glass darkly because we are situated in a limited time and space in history, because we are individuals or because we are shaped by specific communities. In addition to all these factors, our perspective, our natural view, is also affected by sin. Only modified by the lenses of a God-validated testimony can the meaning of the whole narrative of life become clearer. Indeed, "god, freedom and immortality" is the insightful secular version of the clear and distinct theme/motif/motive of "creation, fall, and recreation" as lodged in the nature of created reality and also set

The Projection of Moses from out of His Own Completed World

forth in the overall narrative of the Bible and as seen through the lens of Scripture.

What other aspects of the projection stand out? There is God and what is totally distinct from him; there is God and the creation, the first and most sacred separation or line of demarcation. Lines of demarcation become extremely prominent in Genesis, as in the entire Elder Testament. In Moses' description of the product of the successive divine, creative delineations there is an amazing architectural arrangement that grounds Moses' life world. The physical world is given first; it is basic and simple, and its realities can be counted and denoted. Then there is motion, and also in succession after that there is life in the form of plants, vegetation and fruits. Living things are produced by other living things. Then in the acts of God, the great separation maker, the *hamabdil* of Gen 1, there are animals that come from animals for all anyone has ever observed.

Finally, there are humans, male and female, created as distinct beings after their own kind, who produce other human beings, for all anyone has ever evidenced and for all anyone has ever seen, known, or experienced. Nothing else produces human beings, except other human beings. We can trust what we see and experience. The fanciful addition of inconceivable stretches of "time" does not help like magic to alter the basic picture. This is the multifaceted world of Moses' present. That world is trustworthy as experienced day by day, and thus for Moses that world is received from the hand of God as in the beginning, *for all anyone can ever know*. Moses is truly our first genuine commonsense realist.

Following this account of Moses we must begin there and then stop there before moving forward with the subsequent story of sin as it is told in Gen 2:4b—3:24. Contrary to the widespread historical-critical theory of Wellhausen, we need not construe Gen 2:4b—3:24 as a *second* creation story. Wellhausen made this claim because in chapter 1 God is referred to as Elohim, while in chapter 2:4b—3:24 the name of God changes to Jahweh.[1] I would assert that the difference between chapter 1 and 2:4b—3:24 is not just the difference of the names by which God is called. Rather the major difference is that chapter 1 is the story of creation and chapter 2:4b—3:24 includes the story of the *fall* as well.

The long narrative of sin and salvation, the life of God's chosen people being urged to live in obedience to the divine wisdom is the continuation of Moses' narrative. He chooses not to delve into the unknown of what

---

1. Wikipedia, "Julius Wellhausen."

was before it all. He chooses not to speculate about what God was thinking/planning/decreeing before he created the cosmos; nor does Moses try to figure out exactly how God did it. For Moses, as also for us, for all we can ever know, the world God founded and grounded is roughly the world as we experience it. With this established, with the stage now set, the rest of the story, the *toledoth*, is ready to begin. Begin there because there is enough to consider about human history from that point *forward* to keep all of us completely occupied, without giving way to "vain speculation," as Calvin at his best so frequently cautioned.

CHAPTER 5

What We Learn from Genesis 1 and 2

A. AGAINST SPECULATION

As a Calvinist, I wish to offer a few cautionary comments about the matter of original creation and how we learn about it. Just as theologians like to speculate, to go beyond God's works and Word in talking about creation, so human thought in general likes to do the same, including that which takes place in philosophy and especially in our day in the natural sciences. Scientific speculations seem more and more to be inspired by exotic science fiction.[1] The assumption seems to be that if we can get behind the creation as we have it and know it in its diversity and variety, then we can trace the steps of its coming into being and thus come closer to discovering the key to its mystery. In doing that, could we then in some sense be said to create the world ourselves because our power over things is god-like? For moderns tracing the steps of a thing's becoming is tantamount to being the thing's lord and master, or at least the next best thing to being its creator. One might wonder if this is on the near horizon with rapidly developing AI.

As we approach the question of original creation, even asking what Scripture tells us about it, we must ever be aware of the fact that it is shrouded in unfathomable mystery. This point has already been stressed in the previous chapter, but it bears repeating. The further back we go in our thoughts about it, the more we draw a blank, just as we do in our own personal lives. To know anything about our own early lives we depend on stories that are told to us by others. To know anything about creation we are

---

1. Midgley, *Evolution as a Religion*, 29–39.

dependent on the story that God tells us about it. The story is not science, but it is populated with truth claims nonetheless. We cannot properly contemplate God's works apart from that story, as it provides the indispensable framework, a set of control beliefs, for the scientific study of creation. As Calvin once put it:

> Let this admonition, no less grave than severe, restrain the wantonness that tickles man and even drives to wicked and hurtful speculations. In short, let us remember that that invisible God, whose wisdom, power, and righteousness are incomprehensible, sets before us Moses' history as a mirror in which his living likeness glows. For just as eyes, when dimmed with age or weakness or by some other defect, unless aided by spectacles, discern nothing distinctly; so, such is our feebleness. Unless Scripture guides us in seeking God, we are immediately confused. They who, indeed, indulge their wantonness, since they are now warned in vain, will feel too late by a dreadful ruin how much better it would have been for them reverently to accept God's secret purposes than to belch forth blasphemies by which to obscure heaven. And Augustine rightly complains that wrong is done God when a higher cause of things than his will is demanded.... To gratify their curiosity, they strive to go forth outside the world. As if in the vast circle of heaven and earth enough things do not present themselves to engross all our senses with their incomprehensible brightness.... Therefore let us willingly remain enclosed within these bounds to which God has willed to confine us, and as it were, to pen up our minds that they may not, through their very freedom to wander, go astray.[2]

B. THE CREATOR-CREATION DISTINCTION

It is significant that the Bible begins its story with the beginning of creation and *not* with God. What the Bible does not do or what the Bible does not say (about what God was doing, thinking, and planning "before" he created) tells us volumes about how the Bible views the relationship between God and what he created. As Angelo Rappoport says in his *Myths and Legends of Ancient Israel*:

> Unlike the myths of other nations ... Jewish myth deals but little with the origin of God. He was there before the mountains were

2. Calvin, *Institutes* 1.14.1.

born, before the world was created, and from the beginning of time to the end of days He exists and is God. Since time immemorial His throne is established. Jewish myth makers . . . refrain from inquiring into the mysteries of Divinity . . . . God was, has been, and is, and that was sufficient even for those who indulged in creating and fashioning the myths of Israel. Therein consists the difference between the myths of Israel and those of other nations who relate the birth of the respective Gods.[3]

The coming into being of the creation is not a part of a story about God or the gods. In the Bible cosmogony is not a subordinate part of theogony, as in the myths of the ancient Near East. There is a stable order or difference between God and what is not god in the Bible. The boundary between the two is not fluid, and so God does not exemplify the behavior of earthlings. Moreover, things that are not god are made, not begotten; creation is not pro-creation. Nor for that matter is there anything in the world that is divine or worthy of worship. From what the Bible assumes about the Creator-creation relationship, we learn that creation is wholly relative to and dependent on God, that its status is that of creature rather than creator. Whatever is not god is dependent, subordinate, and humble in comparison to God, the almighty maker of heaven and earth, i.e., of all things invisible and visible.

C. YET ALL IS VERY GOOD

Even though nothing in the world is worthy of worship or is over humans, everything created is very good. The biblical account does not let us forget that. In the Bible there is no metaphysical analogy or comparison between God and creation, but there is an analogy or comparison between the world as created and creation as God intended it to be in the beginning. In the original creation all things were conformed to the purpose and will of God for how they should be.

All things as created were able to perform the will of God perfectly. That is implicit in the pronouncement that they are "very good" in the beginning. That is what it means too that humans were created in the image of God. There was unity between God and creation, a harmony of purpose, a coincidence of wills between God and humans. There was peace between

---

3 Rappoport, *Myths and Legends*, 1–2.

Creation as an Introduction to Christian Thought

heaven and earth. In the beginning this is a first perfect creation from which to fall.

Human beings by power of natural reason alone are incapable of fully accounting on their own for the perfectly good creation. There is the Bible's Eden and later Milton's Paradise Lost, and Jesus' reference to Paradise as he speaks to the thief on the cross next to him when he was crucified. In the biblical narrative there are Adam and Eve, the two progenitors of the human race, and there was a fall from the original state of rectitude that existed before. Natural reason left on its own can only come up with "it's always been like it is now." In fact, also the idea of an absolute beginning or that "time" had a "beginning" is beyond the capacity of fallen natural reason to come up with.

In the original creation there is no in-built deficiency. What is broken or flawed in the world as we have it was not a part of the original order of things; it was not a natural part of life. The Bible views the bad as an intruder, as out of place in God's creation. The remedy in Scripture—let us say "salvation" for the moment—is always the *restoration* of creation rather than its eclipse or a departure from out of it through death, as suggested by Plato. There are many ways to "pidginize" and pooh-pooh creation.

If we had our way, if we could have it the way we would think about things without scriptural revelation, good and evil would always have existed together. Modern secular thought often goes there. For example, Elizabeth Gilbert in her novel *The City of Girls* suggests in humor that without some transgression, the world would be a rather boring place.[4] Just as we cannot think light without darkness, so we cannot think good without evil, since no one has experienced such a condition. Only with the aid of Scripture can we know about a paradise lost. Our ancestors only knew of a world in which both good and evil, life and death, coexisted. The case is the same for their ancestors in turn, and so it was as far back as we can go using ordinary human history and memory. That is where the secular world, in fact, leaves it. Good and evil seem to be two sides of the same coin, coequal or equally ultimate. This is not so for Scripture.

A world in which good and evil do not exist alongside one another is unthinkable. It is unacceptable for natural reason and for ordinary biblically uninformed experience to imagine. Yet Scripture tells that it was once not so and thus that it was once entirely different. Original creation was simply only "very good," and it was this first, in the *beginning*. Good came

---

4. Gilbert, *City of Girls*.

What We Learn from Genesis 1 and 2

first and then only later did evil appear in connection with the creatures of God. Good belongs to the foundation; evil and its remedy only to subsequent history.

Good and evil are not coequal; evil is not a natural aspect of things; death is not a natural part of life, which is why all human beings instinctively fight against it with goodly vigor. These things are not all a part of the process, as evolutionistic theory assumes. In the biblical view very goodness can even exist without evil; it does not need it. Evil is secondary, an intruder, or a parasite. It needs the good upon which to reap its havoc. Evil comes *after* the good (after Gen 1:1—2:4b) and can only be in relation to it and dependent on it. All of that is in the idea, the declaration, that in the beginning things were very good.

But there is more. The whole creation as created is only very good. Nothing is unclean in itself. As the Bible treats the problem of evil, it continues to view the world with intrinsic admiration. The world order is not to blame for our problems. It isn't the woman God gave us, and we have no right to blame it on the snake. We have no reason to use the tragically common habit of blaming the circumstances in which we find ourselves. Imperfection does not inhere in our circumstances.

CHAPTER 6

Creation as Separation

ALREADY IN OUR REFLECTIONS on the most initial creation claims of the Gen 1:1—2:4b text, I have emphasized the separation of Creator from the creation. The distinction is absolute. The narrative assumes that the creation had a beginning. By no means do all creation myths assume that, as we shall see from modern versions of "origins." The most prominent concept associated closely with the beginning narrative in Scripture is what traditionally has been called *creatio ex nihilo*, or "creation out of nothing." The most closely affiliated idea of *creatio continua*, or "continuing creation" is also present, although it might better be described as "preservation." The two are not the same, as the terms would indicate. But the story of the text surely stresses the former as first and foundational.

A. CREATION OUT OF NOTHING

In modern theology excessive effort has been put into establishing a close affiliation between "creation out of nothing" and "ongoing creation." Blurring the distinction between the two has become an obsession in contemporary theology, to such a degree that many have been pushing it to the eschatological end. In the nineteenth century Schleiermacher regarded "creatio ex nihilo" as a speculative and thus useless concept, bearing no real connection with our *immediate* consciousness of absolute dependence.[1] Other

---

1. Schleiermacher, *Christian Faith*, 142–46.

thinkers refer to places elsewhere in Scripture outside of Gen 1:1—2:4b where the text includes references to creation. There are many such texts.

These other references to creation, however, involve the presence of the great disruption brought about by the willful transgression of God's creatures. For one reason or another the careful distinction between the two aspects of creation has fallen into disfavor. In some instances the move is made to pidginize the Elder Testament as Judaistic and judgmental. In other instances there is a push to "Christocratize" or "futurize" everything in the Bible. What has happened to the Christian view of nature or creation? In the secular world and now even within Christianity itself a shift has come about in an effort to accommodate mega-evolutionistic themes thought clearly to have been established "scientifically" as fact. We shall have more to say about this minimization and eclipse of creation in modern theology in the final chapter.

The belief claims implicit in the creation narrative in Gen 1:1—2:4b most clearly entail the *ex nihilo* act. There is God and "then" there is the not god. The two are *separate* and distinct. All the classical translations of the original Hebrew manuscripts, including the Greek Septuagint, the Latin Vulgate, the English King James, RSV, and the NIV, say, "In the beginning God created the heavens and the earth." In Hebraic thought "the heavens and the earth" is the way to refer to everything that is. In effect, this narrative belief claim introduces the entire narrative that follows. Though numerous modern text and historical critics prefer to read the opening as a circumstantial rather than substantive clause ("when . . ."), several prominent modern scholars continue to insist on the millennia-long, majority, and therefore traditional reading. I agree with them.[2]

Another quite fantastic approach has been the claim by Karl Barth that the "nothingness" out of which God created the cosmos was actually "something," i.e., a "reality of sorts" that threatened creation as that into which creation could collapse if God were not there "*to save it*."[3] The latter represents the introduction of yet a new myth to prevent the article of faith concerning creation to stand on its own prior to and outside of the occurrence of the revelation of salvation history. That revelation for salvation, for Karl Barth, represents *all* of Scripture from start to finish, from beginning to end. "There never was a golden age," says Barth. "There is no point

---

2. Westermann, *Genesis 1–11*, 94–95.
3. Barth, *Church Dogmatics*, 3/3:349–50.

in looking back to one. The first man was immediately the first sinner."[4] I shall return to Barth's Christological Unitarianism later in a more extended exploration when we consider the "eclipse of creation" in modern theology.

Creation as origination should be viewed as such as an *ex nihilo* act. Some may disagree that the text of Genesis starts with that, assuming, as they tongue in cheek must, that there had already been an unmentioned prior creation of the "waste and void," or the "chaos." Needless to say, that putative story is most emphatically not the one placed first in the canon of the Elder Testament. To draw on this other unknown story is to suggest that the turtle of our creation story in Gen 1 is standing on the back of another not yet mentioned but more original turtle.

In any case it is difficult to disagree that at least the Christian idea of the creation of everything should have started there, even if the author, the canonizers, and 99 percent of Christian interpreters over the span of two thousand years did not know that there had already been an unmentioned first creation of the "waste and void." In the twentieth century the other prior "creation" got slipped into the narrative implicitly with a "When" and a comma added to the first independent sentence, turning it into a circumstantial clause. Who says that "biblical" theologians are humorless?

Central to this first biblical claim of creation out of nothing, this "prolegomenon," is the establishment of a fundamental distinction of God from the not-god, to what has been called into being by God. Creation out of nothing concerns especially that "moment," or "point," that essentially indescribable and ineffable "x," at which there ceased to be just God. That great "x" designates the point at which God decided to act outside of himself and in relation to a first not-god.

For God things have never been the same since. What we say about that "x," that "moment," and the *separation* established and determined by God with the not-god, lays the ground plan not only for the narrative of Gen 1:1—2:4b but also for the entirety of Christian thought. What is "transcendence," the "transcendence" of God? What is "immanence"? What is the connection between the two? What we say at this point will determine our conception of God and our conception of his relationship to the laws and principles of the world, as well as our view of the nature and limits of human knowledge and our language about God. We shall not go into all of that here, but it is important to make clear that what gets said about these matters "in the beginning" of creation and in the beginning of our

---

4. Barth, *Church Dogmatics*, 4/1:509.

reflections on creation will set a significant model for what immediately follows in the text of Gen 1 and also for the development of subsequent Christian and biblical teachings.

A good example of the uncompromised importance of the creation is how, way down the line, the dynamic of salvation becomes conceived in Christian thought. God saves always in terms of creation, not outside of or above and beyond it, but in a way that does not predetermine it but incorporates and vindicates it. Christian thought in its orthodox and theocentric form lays great emphasis on the sovereignty of God in salvation and the corresponding dependence of human beings. Indeed in the last two thousand years Jesus Christ and the salvation of human beings has been a dominant theme in Christian thought. This doctrine places great stress on the absolute priority of grace and the corresponding unqualified necessity of salvation. The word "alone" became the hallmark of Protestant theology and is thus also today acknowledged by the Catholic Church. The notion that there is nothing of spiritual goodness remaining in humans to accomplish the required radical reorientation is a much-heralded biblical insistence.

From the narrative of creation as an absolute act, we know about the sovereignty and power of God, who is called in the ecumenical creeds of the Christian church "the Father, Almighty, Maker of Heaven and Earth," the "*pantocrator*," to use the exact word of the Septuagint. God's *potentia*, as expressed in the Latin Vulgate, is unlimited. The assumption of the creation portrayal in Gen 1 is that God and the not-god are *sui generis* and unique; there exists between them no natural analogy, no connection that does not require a corresponding divine *choice* to condescend, accommodate, and reveal. *In principium*, God and the not-god are unqualifiedly and exhaustively distinct; the first *opera ad extra* of God is portrayed as an absolute act. This is also designated by the Hebrew terms "*bara*" and "*hamabdil*" in Genesis.

The act of God in creation is not subject to or determined by any condition. Within the determinate system of things, nothing comes from nothing. But since something has come from and out of nothing, according to Christian teaching concerning creation, God and the act of God whereby a relationship is established with the *ad extra* do not belong to the determinate or conditioned system of things. The creation of the world took place outside of, apart from, and beyond the world itself.

Creation as an Introduction to Christian Thought

The divine action of separating himself out from all of what was created is the origin of all determinations and conditions and is therefore absolute. Calvin states it in this way: because Moses used the verb "*bara*" to designate creation, "therefore his meaning is that the world was made out of nothing."[5] God's act of creation is itself an unconditioned act in the absolute sense. This is an idea that brings us to the very limit of our understanding and language, for we can by the nature of the case only think and refer to the indeterminate in determinate terms, the very determinate terms brought into being by the indeterminate act of God in creation.

In the earliest Christian teachings concerning creation, there is great resistance to viewing God's creation as a response to an already existing "something." This is an especially strong contrast to what we see in classical philosophy. *Creatio* is not *formatio* or *techne*. It is *not* a demiurgic response to a matter ripe with potentiality. God not only shapes the universe out of matter according to some logical "forms"; he not only creates the "matter" (existence) of the universe out of nothing; but he also creates the "form" (essence) of the universe. God not only brings the universe into being with a determinate plan, but he creates the principles whereby the universe is given a determinate nature and form. And, finally, God not only creates the very first principles of the world; he even creates all of the abstract logical possibilities of which the "forms" are specific instances.

We need to exercise extreme caution in thinking in terms of "matter" and "form" and logical possibilities when we think about creation! Even if we were to concede, for the moment, to the use of these specifically pagan and nonbiblical notions, we would say that they too are determinate and belong to the system of things that God created out of nothing, so that before, and beyond, and outside of creation, they simply were *not*.[6]

Before moving on from this point, it is important to emphasize that creation out of nothing does not, of course, deny constraint or necessity. The question with regard to constraint and necessity is the nature of that necessity within the framework of the truth of creation. Naturally there can be no necessity as such, obtaining even for God as such. Who in the world do humans think they are that they would even dare to say what is necessary for God?

In any case, apart from the hubris of saying what necessity might mean for God, we would allow, and even argue strongly for the idea of a created

---

5. Calvin, *Commentaries on Genesis*, 70.
6. Clouser, *Myth of Religious Neutrality*, 43–45.

or ordained necessity. *Given creation*, there is a determinate order to which God has committed himself and according to which he has bound himself to work and to be talked about, as Scripture does. We can count on that.

We might make many concessions to those who have spoken about necessity, if what has been said about it were confined to the product of God's free act and enclosed *within* its limits. What cannot be reconciled with creation out of nothing is the idea that necessity is absolute, so that it applies both to God and the not-god, or so that it applies to God apart from any act and product of God's creating.

B. CREATION AND PRESERVATION

In Genesis, Moses' creation story teaches absolute creation and the establishment of a creation order. Moses has looked at the complex world in which he lives and, since no human was present at the beginning event, Moses simply avers that the world of his native experience is the world received from the hand of God in the beginning, for all anyone can ever know.

Thus far in our discussion here of creation out of nothing, we have touched on the following elements, which are summarized here for the sake of clarity.

First, *creatio ex nihilo* posits an act of creation outside of time, and thus it expresses the conviction that in creating God is absolutely free. A corollary of this is the assumption that ontically Creator and creature are absolutely separate and, therefore, a boundary or separation between God and "the heavens and the earth" must be accepted. The fundamentally biblical and Christian contention, that in being God and the cosmos are noncoincidental, is basic to Christian truth.

A second element present in the positing of an act of creation that takes place outside of time is the implication that the act of creation is itself not a temporal process. Accordingly, the idea of a creation out of nothing invariably necessitates the discrimination of an original free act of creation outside of time and a temporal process of becoming that is the unfolding of an order already established and created. We have creation out of nothing in Gen 1:1—2:4b and we have the preservation and unfolding of that order in chapter 2:4b—3:24.

Positing a *creatio ex nihilo* introduces us at this point to a third ingredient of the doctrine of creation. The fact that the act of creation is not a

Creation as an Introduction to Christian Thought

temporal event or process implies that creation in its original sense was an absolutely free creative act (*bara*) that was finished and completed. It was a once-for-all act that was followed by the temporal process of the unfolding of a created order of separated entities and things. God did not cease to be present to his creation. To say that he ceased to be present is a Deistic distortion, and it leads to reductions of the idea of creation to "reality," "nature," or simply "world."

It is appropriate to follow here with the traditional notion of *creatio continua* as preservation.

It is a Christian truth claim that all creatures owe the continuance and development of their existence to the will and uninterrupted exercise of the power of God. They do not owe it to any inherent principle of being. Creation is not "nature," in the sense of a natural order that is grounded in a principle inherent in itself. Apart from God, the creation would collapse into nonexistence. God creates a determinate reality of separated orders, but the preservation of the creation is due ultimately to the constancy and faithfulness of God himself. After the establishment of a created order, human beings and God's other creatures took up their respective tasks and roles in pursuance of the cultural mandate (Gen 1:28).

We must resist the temptation to confound creation and preservation by reducing creation to continuing divine presence, as much modern theology today is highly prone to do. This latter view is driven by "science" as well as by the hunch that the first perfect creation is an eschatological hope. There are frequent claims that creation out of nothing is not present in Gen 1. The argument rests on other, later texts in Scripture having to do with *ex nihilo* creation, which texts are then taken to be just as important as Gen 1. From these passages it is concluded that there needs to be a constant upscaling, commonly called "evolution," going on in the world, and it needs to be accommodated in our thinking.

There is an essential question that needs to be raised here. Is it "upscaling" or "collapsing"? Because I am not willing to change biblical teaching to accommodate current scientific trends, I continue to assert, in defense of *creatio ex nihilo* and preservation, that the former is the calling into a real, nondivine order what before did not exist, and the latter is "the continuing and causing to develop" of that new order.[7] It is also appropriate to

---

7. I find it helpful to use the Dutch term here for that event of calling into being something that before did not exist. It is *"ontstaan"* and it is a term distinct from the one that is used to reference "continuing and causing to develop," which is *"bestaan."*

ask whether what follows the original creation described in Gen 1:1—2:4b should even be called a form of creation, which is what the term "*creatio continua*" suggests. Might it be that "providence" or "preservation" would be clearer and more appropriate terms with which to designate this ongoing care of God for the creation?

C. CREATION AS SEPARATION/DIVISION/ DIFFERENTIATION

What comes next is at the heart of Moses' creation saga, as projected from the retrospective glance of his own life world. If the Scripture is both divine *and human*, this is the best God's human creatures could have done, showing not only what the reality of God's creation was "in the beginning" but also the saga's being transparent with regard to its "for all anyone can ever know" status.

The analysis of Gen 1 that follows is presented as an interpretation of the text that intends to honor the overall import of it. I shall attempt an interpretation that is attentive to the stated topic of this chapter, i.e., creation as separation and differentiation. The status of differences, qualities, and distinguishing characteristics among God's creatures is an issue in the foreground of Gen 1.

I would say that the text of Gen 1 is about the world as accessible to ordinary human beings just as the world that Moses describes and in which he lived was accessible to him. It is as if the author of the text were natively reflecting on the completed and marvelously rich world of his own immediate experience, the infinitely diverse and yet intricately interconnected world of water and sea, plants and animals, and men and women. The text *implies*, in fact, that this world is the only world about which we can speak respectably, for it suggests through its mode of portrayal that our thinking must begin and end with that world. Our thinking should not go beyond it, behind it, or beneath it. Significantly it is the world of everyday life that the text and its author, Moses, present to us. It is the world as accessible to humans in the wholeness of their existence with its experienced multiplicity of entities and things.

My emphasis at this point is part of a long exegetical tradition. It can be found in Augustine as he explains the text of Gen 1 in chapters 11–13 of the *Confessions*. Luther and Calvin also belong in this tradition, a fact that helps in understanding their constant warning against speculation and arbitrary thinking. For example, commenting on the first several verses of Gen 1, Calvin remarks, "It must be remembered that Moses does not speak with philosophical acuteness on occult mysteries, but related those things which are everywhere observed, even by the uncultivated, and which are in common use." Later, in the same vein, he continues with a description of the text's linguistic mode as commonsensical and realistic:

> For Moses addresses himself to our senses, that the knowledge of the gifts of God which we enjoy may not glide away. Therefore, in order to apprehend the meaning of Moses, it is to no purpose to soar above the heavens; let us only open our eyes to behold this light which God enkindles for us in the earth. By this method the dishonesty of those men is sufficiently rebuked who censure Moses for not speaking with greater exactness. For as he became a theologian, he had respect to us rather than to the stars. Moses wrote in a popular style things which, without instruction, all ordinary persons endued with common sense are able to understand; but astronomers investigate with great labor whatever the sagacity of the human mind can comprehend.[8]

Not only does the text speak in such a way that, as Luther says again and again, the uneducated can easily understand it if they attend to the plain and simple sense,[9] but it also dares to call this phenomenal world and permanently given whole *"the beginning."*

This means, for one thing, the thinking of redeemed persons wearing the spectacles of the Scriptures must begin with the world as given in immediate experience and as described by the Genesis story of creation. For redeemed thinking this is the least arbitrary approach.

Luther and Calvin both frequently argue that it is the mark of unredeemed thinking to inquire into lofty matters without God's Word or works. Such persons, Luther continues, do their thinking about God and what is beyond creation "with the same sureness with which they argue about a pig or cow.... They exert themselves to ascend to heaven without ladders, that is, without the Word . . . and fall to their destruction." Therefore, Luther continues, "if we want to walk safely, let us accept what the Word submits for our reflection and what God himself wants us to know."[10]

---

8. Calvin, *Commentaries on Genesis*, 85–86.
9. Luther, *Lectures on Genesis*.
10. Luther, *Lectures on Genesis*, 13–14.

Creation as Separation

Dietrich Bonhoeffer points out so well that it is a bold challenge to our "natural" reason that the text calls the phenomenally given whole described in the first chapter *"the beginning."*[11] Without the biblical revelation our reason thinks backward from the things that are given and can reach no beginning. On its own it can only reach an eternally given present and an eternal return. Some thinkers in the "Christian" tradition have asserted an eternal creation, or the idea of a time that has no beginning so that God himself is thought to be within it absolutely. The early church father Origen was severely rebuked by the church for giving in to this notion of eternal creation.[12]

"In the beginning God created the heavens and the earth." Scripture accepts God's existence as self-evident; it begins with the immediate awareness of God's existence and does not try to justify his life to our thinking. In this way Gen 1 makes its most basic religious decision, grounding one of the foundational beliefs of the Christian faith, namely that God and the creation are absolutely separate and qualitatively different.

In the Reformed tradition this belief has come to expression under the rubric of the sovereignty of God. For example, articulating his conception of God's sovereignty, Abraham Kuyper stresses throughout his works the boundary between God and his creatures. This is an especially prominent theme in Kuyper's *De Verflauwing der Grenzen* (*The Blurring of the Boundaries*), where he mentions again and again that "between God and the world there exists the sharpest boundary" (*"tusschen God en de wereld [ligt] . . . de scherpste grenslijn"*). So we see that the creation story is grounded in an assumption that permeates the entire Elder Testament witness: God is infinitely qualitatively different than his works. The basic differentiation of all things, according to Kuyper, is "the distinction that is the mother of all others" or *"moedertegenstelling."*[13] It is the distinction by which God places himself "over against" his creation. This difference is the one that is at the beginning/birthing of everything else; it is the difference most inviolable and fundamental to Christian faith and distinguishes Christianity from its pagan alternatives.

---

11. Bonhoeffer, *Creation and Fall*, 13–20.

12. Later Thomas Aquinas also lent credibility and support to this idea, but he was perceptive enough to make clear that this conclusion is reached by purely natural or autonomous reason.

13. Kuyper, *Verflauwing der Grenzen*, 8. Tr. H. vd. Goot.

Creation as an Introduction to Christian Thought

Note too, and now especially, that this concept of separation sets a pattern! Creator and creation are not to be confused. There is a created order, a law order of creation. There are creation ordinances. Not only are they separate and distinct in kind; things in the world are also separate and distinct from each other in kind. We experience this to be the case as did Moses, given the limits of where he found himself as author of the narrative. Again to use the words of Abraham Kuyper:

> That man should ever be aware of the fundamental boundary-line between God and creation, God thought it fitting to reflect that boundary-line in the firm boundaries that he established among his creatures . . . (i.e.,) God ordered separations among all his creatures as an expression of the absolute separation that he maintains between creation and himself.[14]

God and creation are not the only terms separated from one another. The idea of separation and division is a prominent theme throughout the first chapter of Genesis as the cosmos is being established, laid down, founded, and described. In fact this conceptuality controls much of the further presentation of material in the first chapter of Genesis.

The third verse of the first chapter of Genesis announces the introduction of the Word. It is interesting to note that with the Word's appearance there is a commencement of distinguishing, which is one of the Word's unique functions. In fact the term "separate" (*hamabdil*) appears five times in the text after this point and ten times in expressions like "after its kind" (*lemino*), which is naturally used in Moses' portrayal as a commonsense category rather than a scientific concept. As Leo Strauss, a scholar of classical Hebrew texts, argues, to the Hebrew reader "creation is the making of separated things, of species of plants, animals, and so on; creation means even the making of separating things—heaven separates water from water, the heavenly bodies separate day from night,"[15] etc., as the account continues.

Allow me to illustrate this from the text of Gen 1. Clearly God's activity is essentially one of separation and distribution. In verse 4, for example, light is separated from darkness. Furthermore, the things distinguished each have a unique duty, for the entities separated are immediately named: the light is called "day" and the darkness "night." This pattern of separation is closely linked with the establishment of an identity or "name" as that is

14. Kuyper, *Ijzer en Leem*, 11–12. Tr. H. vd. Goot.
15. Strauss, "Interpretation of Genesis."

understood in Hebrew thought. One's "name" among the Hebrews functions like the "soul" for the Greeks. This first segment ends by associating the two related things with what the author calls "one day," as if in reference to a category and not simply a time frame.

In the next segment of the text a similar activity and product are mentioned. An expanse called "sky" is ordained to separate "the waters above from the water under" it. A boundary or limit is established as a "firmament," that is, an indelible line of demarcation, so that what is above should never be commingled with what is below. It appears that Moses views the mixing of such experientially different orders, what is above and what is below, as a serious threat. Moreover, this activity of separating (*hamabdil*) and its product are again associated with what the author calls a "second day," or topic.

In the following segment God creates the sea and separates it from dry land in the waters under the sky, thus continuing his work of division and specification. But an interesting new note is added with respect to the segregated earth, namely that God calls it to bring forth its own produce. With this act of creation/separation the thing created is endowed with lawful self-activity. God does not directly bestow on humans and beasts their sustenance; rather, he works through the agency of the earth, which carries forth this process. By his Word God establishes in the beginning, but only through the creature does he continue his work of bestowing goodness and life on all. Calvin was fond of saying in his commentary on Genesis that there is a persistent closeness to commonsense experience in the text.

Near the conclusion of the third segment, the author states that the plants of the earth brought forth fruit, "each according to its kind." Again, Moses is talking commonsense experience. Native experience is reliable, trustworthy. When plants produce other plants, this is not a deception or a cover up for some other continuous process. Where the language of separation and division is not used, the idea emerges that God created "kinds," which regularly produce according to the laws of their own existence and calling. Moses is not proposing a primitive science; rather he is simply taking the world in which he lives for what it is, for how human beings experience it, without any doubts. To know the "how" of their genesis beyond this calling of them into being is assumed to be beyond our reach. For Moses the only real certainty is not the reductionist "I think; therefore I am." Sorry Mr. Descartes. For Moses the truth of the matter is "I see; therefore I know." And, again, segment three closes with "And God *saw* that it was good."

Segment four recounts the creation/separation of the heavenly bodies: sun, moon, and stars. Again, as day is separated from night and light from darkness, the sun, moon, and stars are distinguished from one another. Furthermore, this arrangement is a well-ordered whole, a planetary rhythm that humans are called to emulate in their daily lives; for the lights of the heavens are to be "for signs and seasons and for days and years." The arrangement of life in a coherent unity, including the distinctly human order of history and culture, is reflected by the physical and astronomical patterns of the universe. Finally, segment four also ends with the identification of the fourth day and the assertion that "God saw that it was good." By now how could any reader miss that last point?

The fifth segment announces the creation of animals, each according to its kind. Again, as in verse 11 where the earth is commissioned to put forth fruit, so here the beasts of the sea and the birds of the air are ordered to be fruitful and multiply. Note that their continued reproduction is viewed as a self-activity. Finally, the segment ends with a designation of it as the "fifth day."

The sixth segment marks a crucial juncture in the text of Gen 1. First, animals that inhabit the dry ground are brought forth according to the divine Word. Noteworthy is the triple mention of their creation "each according to its kind." Surely the author wishes to stress that the phenomenal world, with all of its tacitly experienced basic differences, is a given whole, an established order, at least for all anyone can ever know. Humans cannot get *behind* God's creation. Moreover, the idea that each is created "according to its kind" serves not only to express the separate and specific existence of creatures endowed with generic "identities" but serves as well to indicate their maintenance in such a state. The creation is not a totally fluid order, for self-active beings only produce "according to their kind," thereby ensuring their continued existence according to the law of their callings. There is no natural processive escalator here that leads naturally to the next creatures cited in segment six.

Central to segment six is the story of the creation of humans in the image of God, a narrative element that represents the penultimate high point of the creation saga. Important is that God created human beings as male and female, a differentiation established in the foundational creation order. "Male" and "female" are not just culturally conditioned ideas that humans have come up with. The truth claim here is about as far from the notion that sexual identity is a social construct as one could possibly get. It is a claim that validates common human experience, modern cultural machinations to the contrary notwithstanding. These machinations and human actions in accordance with them will gradually begin to show their incompatibility with the Tao of creation.

Because gender is the only personal quality mentioned in the text, the difference between male and female is seen as being the basic distinction among persons. In this very distinction the text roots a fundamental part of its tripartite commission or mandate "to be fruitful and multiply, and to fill the earth, and to have dominion over it." Modern theologians and biblical scholars are constantly trying to mellow this mandate of Gen 1:28 and to talk it away. If humans follow the mandate, they will be blessed; and after the fall, we see that if humans do not follow the mandate, they will be "cursed." This is the story of Cain and his lineage as well as the story of Babel.

Out of the order of humans created as male and female arises the procreative order of marriage and family. And, at last, out of the family and on its basis, the commission to subdue the earth and have dominion over it is made possible. Blessing is viewed as a *consequence* of the mandate followed. The blessing comes second, after the mandate, not first. There is a frequent confusion in this regard by those who wish to soften the mandate's intent by calling the interaction between God and humans a "blessing." It is hard to ignore the Hebraic and Elder Testament law idea (Torah) in the original creation. Indeed, the cultural mandate may have been abused in the much later course of Western civilization; however, it is anachronistic to attempt to ground so-called eco-theology in the book of Genesis.

One can hardly fail to recognize that the notion of human dominionship stands out vividly in the text. Humans are called to develop and work the garden, not babysit it. The goal is human civilization, and it takes work (the possible meaning of life?) and even some pushing to accomplish that. Consider here again the story of Babel and God's voice in it. In the narrative, the story of the creation of humans in God's image is the narrative's penultimate high point. Just as the "expanse" of verse 6 serves the heavens above and the water beneath, so the waters serve the dry ground and earth; just as the earth serves plants and animals, so the night serves the moon, and day, the sun. But animals and all things serve humans, the lords of creation. Great emphasis is placed on the human responsibility to supervise the development, according to the order of creation, of what God established in principle in the beginning. Lynn White was right about what the text says, quite wrong about rejecting Christianity's Bible for creating the Western environmental crisis because of the cultural mandate.[16]

Segment seven represents the climax of the story. The initial work of the establishment of the created order is finished; God rests, having blessed and hallowed the seventh day. In the end everything is ordered to the seventh day and hence to the divine purpose. Just as the text begins with God, taking his separate existence for granted, so the text returns to him. God does not create for any purpose other than himself. He does not create to save; he creates for his own honor and glory. As each separate thing or realm of things in creation is ordered into service to that which follows it in creation, so all things together reach their ultimate end in dedication to the Lord of the Sabbath. The goal and principle of fulfillment of the world does not reside within the world itself but is outside of the world in the one from whom and unto whom are all things.[17]

---

16. White, "Historical Roots," 1203–7.
17. Richardson, *Toward an American Theology*, 112–13.

CHAPTER 7

Time as Seven Days/Seven Topics

ONE CANNOT HELP BUT see the prominence throughout the narrative of Gen 1 of the theme of separation and division. Indeed, this motif is so striking that Abraham Kuyper ascribes to God the name "The Separation Maker"[1] in order appropriately to circumscribe his absolute sovereignty as portrayed in the text of Gen 1. At this point it is fitting to add a comment on the text's association of the seven separated orders with the seven "days" of the work-a-day week.

Only in the last five hundred years or so has the interpretation of the notion of "day" in Gen 1 acquired an almost exclusively temporal or durational meaning, possibly because of the emergence of literalism with the rise of modern science. In the early church, however, the difficulties inherent in defining "day" as either an astronomical day of twenty-four hours or a vast geological age or period were well recognized. Questions about how "one day" could be constituted according to verse 5 without sun, moon, and stars, which were not created until day four, supported the search for alternative interpretations. Origen, Hilary, and Augustine are numbered among these novel interpreters.

From the early church, especially from Augustine, we can learn that "time," the "time" of "day" in Gen 1, indicates something far more than duration. Instead of "time" Augustine speaks of "topics."[2] Creation, as I have pointed out, means separation and the identification of distinct realms of things that humans experience as really different. "Day" is thus a distinction

1. Kuyper, *Destruction of Boundaries*.
2. Augustine, *Literal Meaning of Genesis*, 134–45.

in being, in things, or among things rather than merely a distinction in time, if at all.

"Day" and "time" in the ancient Hebrew sense indicate primarily the rich variety and arrangement of behavior. "Day" and "time" represent the cosmic order of succession, that rich diversity of distinct and separate things successively ordered in relation to one another from the simplest physical realities of earth, water, and air to plants, animals, and on to humans, culminating finally in the holiness of the Sabbath. We are confronting here the full world of creation as Moses experienced it in his primary life world, projected, of course, on to the beginning in the absolute sense to indicate the limits of all human knowledge when it comes to the *mysterium tremendum* of the origin itself.

It is as if the author of Gen 1 stepped into the great theater of the universe and proceeded to describe its main stage props while waiting for the drama of history (*toledoth*) to begin with the inception of other developments. He takes special note of all the things that daily surround us, and he views them as rooms of the house of creation in which the years of our lives run their course. This rich creation, he silently declares by the mode of his narrative, is the stage for life and the domicile of human beings; we have received it, and still receive it, from the hands of God, just as we experience it.

In order properly to designate and catalogue the many things that Moses sees in his life world, he chooses the week with its sevenfold design as a device for his presentation. Each distinct order he calls a "day." Within these seven days, seven rooms of the universe, he suggests, humans must make their home. In this world so constituted humans are made to live; from such a beginning humans hail; and unto such an end, properly developed according to the order established in the beginning, they are destined to live their days. From such an end they may fall, and finally to such an end they are destined to be restored. Because creation is first and primary, salvation is the *restoration* of creation rather than its eclipse or its replacement by a heavenly, "second order" kingdom.

Both Luther and Calvin follow this model.[3] Calvin uses the analogy of the theater to describe this most beautiful creation as the third and irreducible factor in the covenant drama that unfolds in the God-human-world chain of our true knowledge. However, Calvin also occasionally used the image of a house. In his commentary on 1 Pet 2:13 he says the following:

---

3. Luther, *Lectures on Genesis*, 36; Calvin, "Commentary on 1 Peter 2," verse 13.

> The verb *ktizein* in Greek . . . means to form or construct a building. Suitable, then is the word "ordination"; by which Peter reminds us, that God the maker of the world has not left the human race in a state of confusion, that they might live after the manner of beasts, but as it were in a building regularly formed, and divided into several compartments. And it is called a *human ordination*, not because it has been invented by men, but because a mode of living, well arranged and duly ordered, is peculiar to men.[4]

Calvin does not tease apart the historical and the literal sense of the text in the manner of many who after the Enlightenment approached it critically. Rather Calvin is accepting that we received the creation and still receive it from the hands of God, just as we experience it in the life world.

Finally, in order properly to designate and catalogue the many things that Moses sees, he chooses the week with its sevenfold quality as his measuring device. Each distinct order he calls a "day." Within these seven days, seven scenes, or seven rooms of the universe, Moses suggests, humans must henceforth find their place and make their home. In this world so constituted male and female were made to live; from such a *beginning* they hail; and finally unto such an end properly developed according to the order established in the beginning they are destined to be restored if salvation were to become necessary. The law of their being is thus with them from the beginning. Human beings are never without the Tao of life; nor for that matter are they being drawn toward it as if it were as yet in the present unknowable. "Time" orders the lives of human beings and by its power supports and directs them on their course and according to its design.

Time, then, in Gen 1 is descriptive of the cross-sectional interrelationship of things in the creation. Among the things God created there is a finely tuned interconnectedness. Everything or every order in life is a cog in a finely tuned machine. The creation ticks with clock-like rhythm and accuracy. Everything is made for everything else: basic nutrients for worms, worms for birds to eat, birds for humans to admire, humans for God to use in the development of his creation. The image of the text is one of an integrally interwoven cosmos of creatures successively serving one another as they together serve the glory of God.

That rhythm, that pulsation constituted by the interaction of distinct things created to fit together is the Bible's view of cosmic time. No modern Reformed thinkers have done more to flesh out the cultural and

---

4. Calvin, *New Testament Commentaries*, 269.

Creation as an Introduction to Christian Thought

philosophical implications of this Elder Testamental conception than Abraham Kuyper and his successor at the Kuyper Institute, Herman Dooyeweerd. Following Kuyper, Dooyeweerd compares the effect of time to a prism through which the light of sun is refracted into different colors. The time that God created in the beginning indicates to Dooyeweerd the intricate coherence of things, the excellence of the rich variety and differentiation in creation, and finally, the sphere sovereignty and modal irreducibility of the orders of creation themselves.[5]

The experienced order and arrangement of different things in the world must not be viewed as alien to being. Scripture, as we have seen, designates exactly this diversity of the phenomenally given whole, *the beginning*, the first principle. The first principle is not, therefore, uniformity and oneness, in which case the multiformity of our experience would be secondary and derivative, moving toward again becoming the One it spiritually is. In the Bible there is no exaltation of homogeneity and sameness, as there is in current secular views of basic identity in which markers of identity have simply become matters of human choice.

Scripture portrays as good the irreducible distinctions among orders, things, and persons within the creation itself. Irreducible distinctions among things in the world are neither accidental appearances in the stream of the "transformation of species" nor mere cultural and social products. That is, they were not absent from the primordial starting point, as evolutionism assumes, nor are they destined to be transcended in a tensionless, eschatological future, as cultural idealism and dialectical materialism assume.

In the biblical idea of the givenness of a creation order diversified according to the seven days, one encounters the very basis of human responsibility. God's sovereignty is such that he creates beings who are distinct from him and that stand "over against" him, having a genuine self-action and lawfulness appropriate to the fulfillment of their own callings and identities. In the Elder Testament this is exemplified in the importance of "names." Langdon Gilkey has astutely observed that Christians may find quite antithetical to their own understanding the view that finite things cannot be separated from God or even from one another. Christian faith asserts, Gilkey rightly continues,

> That creatures are not illusory shadows whose real substance or reality [is] God. Rather each creature [is] a real existent, not

---

5. Dooyeweerd, *New Critique of Theoretical Thought*, 1:102.

identical with God but separate from Him, an existing thing with an intrinsic being, an essential structure, and certain natural powers. Within their fundamental creaturely limits all finite things [are] independent, real, and effective substances able to act among other finite beings, and so able to be a secondary cause of events in space and time. Despite their dependence, contingency, and temporality, creatures possess a given structure of self-activity which determines their reactions and actions amid other finite entities. In man this inherent structure of activity is represented by freedom and intelligence, which enable men to be relatively independent, spontaneous centers of activity within God's world.[6]

Gilkey's remarks are a reminder of the authenticity of the role human authors played even in the composition of Scripture. The same is seen if we consider how, before the civil tribunal of the law, we are all to be treated as "equal" because *in reality outside of the court* we are all beautifully *different*! Last but not least, Gilkey's observation is a reminder that God does not extinguish or undo human cooperation in salvation; those who choose not to be in Christ will pass away, as in Gehenna, forever.

---

6. Gilkey, *Maker of Heaven and Earth*, 60–61.

CHAPTER 8

Separate Structures and Biblical Directives

TO AVOID CERTAIN CONFUSIONS, this is the point in our reflections at which it is necessary to clarify the difference between *biblical directives* and *creational structures*. For example, when Gal 3:25-28 asserts that in Christ we are all "one," and that we are therefore neither "Jew nor Greek, slave nor free, male nor female," we are not forced to choose between unity and "sameness" in Christ, as if that is over against having distinct earthly identities. Appeal to the *directional* principle of unity in Christ cannot determine the *structure* of, for example, government. Both unity in Christ and having earthly identities and structural differences are very good, unity representing God's work in redemption while differences reflect his work in creation.

Oneness in Christ is no alternative to natural separations and differences in this world. In fact, it can be said on the basis of Gal 3 that unity actually only exists concretely in and through the diversity of creation. Stated in general terms, God's act of creation is an act of separation, differentiation, and law giving. The unity of things neither conflicts with differentiation nor represents an alternative to it. In fact, the unity of things is dependent, according to the Christian faith, upon their distinctiveness and differentiation. Christianity refuses to view the unity of things as itself a structural quality among others. Rather, unity or oneness in Christ is the same tendency, push, and dynamic within all the differentiations of human life. Calvin puts it this way: "In as much as these two are very different, we must rightly and conscientiously distinguish them" lest law and gospel continue to be confused.[1]

1. Calvin, *Institutes* 3.19.2.

Separate Structures and Biblical Directives

Although we will return to these matters later in our discussion, for now it is helpful to treat them as warranted control beliefs apparent in the text of Scripture. In a later chapter we will deal more extensively with the eclipse of creation in modern evolutionistic thought. Suffice it to say here, in a preliminary manner, that my reading of Gen 1 conflicts significantly with the myth of evolutionistic science on many levels. When we consider science, we are not just dealing with it as the mirror of nature or as a mere accumulation of the so-called facts. Biblical control beliefs stand in sharp contrast to the worldview control beliefs implicit in the myth of evolutionism. At a later point in our discussion we will illustrate this by turning to the work of several representative thinkers (Midgley, Deloria, and Brown). Let it suffice for our discussion here to observe a few obvious differences between the saga of creation in the Elder Testament and the myth of evolutionism as it dominates many modern sciences today.

Let me say first, as a point of language, that I will only infrequently in this study use the term "evolution." So much damage has been done by the persistent equivocation on this term that in many cases using a substitute term helps to avoid the confusion. For that particular myth and theory prevalent in many sciences, extending from the natural and including the social sciences, I shall use only the term "evolution*ism*." For "evolution" in the ordinary sense of its reference to the occurrence of change over time it is more helpful to refer to it as "differentiation," "development," "complexification," and "mutation" or "adaptation" within species.

For the context of the evolutionistic credo, the formal origin or beginning of the cosmos is singular and simple. The Big Bang Theory does not comport with *creatio ex nihilo*, not by a long shot. In the Big Bang Theory the first principle is a singular material cause, a compact quantum of dust and energy, out of which everything that we know "evolved" and emerged much later. What happens first is not necessarily the cause of what happens next (*Post hoc, ergo propter hoc*). The evolutionistic myth begins with a simple first cause, a compact point of energy or a primordial amoebic glob or maybe even just the law of gravity, according to Stephen Hawking, who has set out the myth for the general reader in his book *Brief Answers to the Big Questions*. "Time" is the second element in the myth, which heals all wounds because it allows for leaping forward to talk about a world that has all of the different entities in it that we now experience and have before us.

In evolutionistic thinking no original order of creation is laid down by God as it is in the narrative of Gen 1:1—2:4b. Rather, differences come later on the escalator through an optimistic view of expansion. Or complexity is taken away on the dump truck of contraction, a more recent and pessimistic view of the universe changing in time. With these conjectures we are in the realm of science fiction, which nonetheless is driving more and more modern visions of trans-human life. The fiction normally asserts that each new and different form of life comes out of the previously existing simpler ones. On this scheme there could not have been a first perfect and roughly complete order of creation. No Paradise Lost, because there never was a Paradise to lose. Everything is reduced to "matter evolving" or "gravity unfolding and/or dissipating." This is most definitely not the storied picture we get from Scripture.

Scripture regards the origin as unknowable, as shrouded in unfathomable mines of never-ending mystery. For the author of Genesis, the beginning is gone and unreachable in itself. The beginning is for Moses in his life world already roughly differentiated according to all kinds of things and the creatures we experience daily as being different from one another. The beginning is a panorama of multiple levels of reality, each governed by its own unique structures and laws. For all anyone can know, the beginning is not a single cause but a cosmic order described according to the scheme of the week, with its seven distinct "days" or topics. When there is development after the original creation, it takes place *within* those realms of things, not from one lower realm to the next higher one in a process of the transformation of the species, speculated but never directly observed. The basic assumptions of the evolutionistic story are not the same as the basic beliefs about creation in the text of Genesis. They represent different *belief* systems.

If there is no absolute beginning, the evolutionistic thinker/believer cannot say that God created the world already, once upon a time. Among so-called "theistic evolutionists" every effort has been made to *soften* the distinction between creation out of nothing and ongoing development (*creatio continua*). Similarly, with no absolute beginning, the evolutionistic or theistic concordist also cannot say that there was a first perfect creation, from which humans fell. In both of these views evil is a natural part of the process of the emergence of reality, in much the same way that death is said to be a natural part of life.

Among "theistic evolutionists" every effort is made to see good and evil as two inescapable parts of the "process." Because there is no complete creation in the beginning from which humans fell, it is meaningless for the

Separate Structures and Biblical Directives

evolutionistic believer to talk about the restoration of creation. We keep on evolving, even into beings higher than ourselves as it is portrayed in science fiction. These fictions also sometimes suggest that we are now beginning the vicious and horrible process of contraction, in which the slow, sure doom of fate falls pitiless and dark. Evolution*ism* works with a basic set of control beliefs entirely different from those found in Scripture.

In the text of Gen 1:1—2:4b there is a connotation of both completeness and of relative recency. "Here it is, what we have received from the hand of God." Not, of course, in all senses of the word "completion" or "recency," but in some very basic sense; the order has been laid down, both structurally in the model of "seven days" and directionally in a cultural mandate. For example, there was no civilization in the garden; that matter God's human creatures were enjoined to cultivate. God's human creatures were given the mission to build and "exercise dominion over" what God had founded. Completeness has to do with the more fundamental elements of experience in Moses' own personal life, as it does also in ours; it has to do with the basic structures and kinds of things with which we are naturally surrounded, which are the only things anyone in our time, as well as in Moses' time, has ever observed consistently, continuously, and basically. The "order" of creation had been established and how to work it had been clearly advised and mandated.

It must be emphasized again that the text of the Bible is theocentric. Its point of view is that of God and the order in which he executed his actions outside of himself. That means quite simply, an original Paradise, lost because of the willful transgression of Adam and Eve in the fall, and then the subsequent, lengthy history of salvation, or rather, restoration. When we focus on the content of the text, the content of what Moses puts forth as God's way of revealing, we see the order in which God chose to act. Admittedly, this does not mean that there is no Christic element in the original creation, even though Gen 1:1—2:4b could not have mentioned it. In the Younger Testament we see several such references. However, even in those cases the function of the second person of the Trinity is mediational, not salvational or restorational. This is a point made clearly by Calvin. The second person of the Trinity *ex-presses* and represents the Father in all of the Father's first person works. When the Father moves outside of himself in creation, that motion is always Christic, i.e., modeling, though not yet mediatorial.

Creation as an Introduction to Christian Thought

The Bible's story is essentially a creation/recreation story. On the face of it the biblical story does not hint at being undergirded and preceded by an alleged *real* story. It gives no passing recognition to another story that is not directly mentioned in the text itself. There is no behind the scenes story about eternity executed in time. There is no mention of the "pre-creational" inner life of God in which the *real* plan and purpose in God's mind was laid down and then subsequently executed in time. In short there is no sufficiently developed textual evidence to support such speculation or game-playing. That kind of pre-story is usually a scenario conjured up in the imagination of systematic theologians who are downplaying their own inadequate sense of the *mysterium tremendum*.

With all of this kept in mind, it is appropriate to say that the story of creation in the beginning is not a story composed, so to speak, when the events recorded actually occurred. That should be fairly self-evident. Nonetheless this is worth mentioning because, in the case of the matter of original creation, it is a more crucial point than any other event recounted in Scripture. Asserting this is a way of holding out against being distracted from the text itself, as we have it before us. We are shifting for a crucial moment to the sometimes distracting matter of Moses' point of view, situation, and contextual circumstances as an aside so that we can clarify the vantage point from which God chose to engage the writer when he wrote. The events the text sets forth are the oldest in history, and the age of the texts themselves are more recent, possibly even more recent than other texts of the Elder Testament.

From this secondary feature of the text we note that the setting that the author of the text presumes is agrarian. The characters are situated in a garden, and they are accompanied by all kinds of creatures and animals. They are enjoined to till and cultivate the earth, to be fruitful and to make babies, and to fill it up. They are enjoined to turn the garden into something more, perhaps eventually a city. This stage of the author's own life in a civilization came later than the original state described in the text. Again, we must emphasize the context out of which Moses is writing. It is the context of the world of his own immediate experience much after the creation was brought into being out of nothing and set in motion from its beginning and origin. The human author was not a witness of the events themselves.

What we are talking about and identifying here is the ordinary world of Moses' experience. That is where the author begins the discourse, his purposeful and God validated projection. How could he, or anyone else for that matter, have begun it anywhere else or in any other way without lapsing into speculation about things he had never experienced or witnessed? Furthermore, how could the saga have been at once both human and divine without such a cooperation of forces? God breathed approval of what Moses wrote!

Moses intimates that the world of his immediate experience is real, that it is not just appearance but reality. The author does not probe extensively as to how it got where it is. Rather he accepts that the world of his own context is essentially, basically, fundamentally the same as the world given/founded in the beginning. Moses thereby acknowledges and intimates the limits of his own understanding with respect to the subject matter at hand, which subject matter is the Origin. The world as we experience it natively, basically, fundamentally, realistically, first hand, is for the author the real world as we have received it from the hand of God in the beginning, at least for all anyone can ever know.

I have emphasized again and again "for all anyone can ever know." Maybe that is the character and flavor of any text or human writing that is also at once about a mystery not witnessed by the author. This is the case even though God has approved the author's projection as an appropriate witness, as good enough. This is not God writing but God providing his witness through Moses, as Moses is in this real-life situation, outfitted with the witness and creation-faith of his more distant ancestors.

This sense of the completeness, the fundamentality of Moses' native experience of his own world, is also coupled with a certain picture of instantaneousness. There is "completeness" to the foundational order laid down by the Creator in his original *creatio ex nihilo*. God speaks and there is. This is a substantial act and result, not a circumstantial one vis-à-vis the "waste and void," the unformed matter of the earth. There is the Word and its performance, as we see it operate so often throughout the Bible. The closest we get, or even can hope to get, to the "how" of original creation is the speaking of God himself. For the rest we are just expected to shut up, to be still and know that God is God.

Once all the speaking of God is done, the creation is there, very similar to the world in which the author of Genesis lived and had his life, with the exception of sin and evil. In this way the author is suggesting that with respect to *original creation*, there is an outer limit to what human beings can know and get at, an outer limit to his and our probing, to his and our curiosity, and to his and our proper place. I must say it: those robed in the cloak of "science," beware! Maybe trying to go way, way back by means of modeling coupled with extrapolation and wishful thinking is not the best use of (the concept of) time.

We are not, and cannot be, talking here about "thought, observation, and experiment" any more, as in the case of the traditional definition of science. Surprisingly, because of its own limits, science describes a multifaceted world without yet having uncovered the connections among the facets discovered. Hope that these connections in the chain of transformation will eventually be discovered is expressed time and again, first by Darwin himself and to the very present day by current evolutionistic scientists and theistic evolutionists.[2] As we say, time will tell. In the case of this quasi-scientific saga extremely long and humanly not experienceable time lines are always in play. Time is the magic trick in evolution*ism*.

The first face of "time" is the vertical structure of the abode of creation, the theater of the divine glory, with its many entities and things in seven days or topics, if you will. This structure characterizes the world arranged in an ascending order of complexity from the simplest, rudimentary elements of air, water, and earth to plants, animals, and finally to human beings themselves. Only in the *second* phase of the unfolding story, often mistakenly called the second creation story (Gen 2:4b—3:24), does the author place the emphasis on moving forward from that point to the story that unfolds with Adam and Eve's fall in the garden. It then moves on to the subsequent and consequent formation of the chosen nation and the heritage of Abraham as the narrative of recreation necessitated by sin and evil. In Gen 1:1—2:4b the story of original creation nears completion, putting aside any opportunity for a behind-the-scenes story about what was really going on in the mind of God before he actually got started.

We should also take note of the fact that the story of Gen 1:1—2:4b is not just about God, or just about human beings, or just about the relationship of the two to one another. There is no simple I and Thou here, as there never is anywhere in the Bible. Sorry Mr. Heidegger. And Mr. Barth too? There is the third element: the world, the cosmos, the garden, "the theatre of the divine glory." Thank you, Mr. Calvin. The theory that the text is essentially "narrative" sometimes is inadequate because of an implicit assumption of I-Thou encounterism. Similarly inadequate is the hint that the "cosmos" in the beginning was no more than a dot or a speck. It is rather, for all we can observe and know from the projection of Moses out of his life

---

2. Crick, *Life Itself*, 88. Cf. also Van Till, *Fourth Day*, 188.

world, a well-ordered whole with a certain home style architecture involving fundamentally different things and rooms, all coming from God and all referencing back to him.

As for the truth claims of this narrative/saga: There is God, who is almighty maker of heaven and earth, and there is the original creation order and arrangement of things. There is an original state of rectitude, indwelt by two human characters, Adam and Eve. And there is subsequently their willful disobedience and fall into sin. These are colossal, radical truth claims embedded in Moses' projection and creation saga. It is simply false and unthinking to imagine that narratives or sagas bear no truth claims within themselves. Similarly it is false and unthinking to imagine that science is the mere collection of facts or a mirror of nature rather than deliberate, abstractive analysis situated within models, paradigms, hunches, and worldviews that shape and are subtly involved in the organization of what is received from the outside.

The world as received from God in the beginning is more than a dot or a speck, or even just a law such as gravity. It is a well-ordered whole with a relatively complete architectural arrangement of many fundamentally different things, all coming from God. The principle of the unity and meaning of all things resides in the transcendent God alone.

The definitive architecture of the building of the cosmos in Gen 1:1—2:4b is highly significant. It comprises all of the basic elements of the vast variety of entities that constitute our environment. It is a slice in "time" that exhibits the order of everything at the beginning. Literature, even fictional literature, communicates the truths that it wishes to speak. So do other kinds of narratives and stories. Narrative is able to express ideas that its texts regard as true. Even myth is not always just fiction. Creation, an original state of rectitude or Paradise, Adam and Eve, the fall into sin, the history of salvation with the birth of the second person of the Trinity, his death on the cross, his resurrection from the dead, and the consummation: these are the *facts* of the biblical narrative as a whole from the beginning to the end. *All of the authors of Scripture thought this way.* Moreover, if the latter salvational elements are considered facts and true by all Christians, e.g., incarnation, cross and resurrection, why not the former, creation-related ones, which too belong to the sequence as a whole from start to finish?

In the original creational scheme the skies open up and expand to more and more similar things. There is so-called matter; there is space; there is motion; there is energy; there are chemicals; there is life and metabolism; there are plants opening up to more and more of their own kind; there are animals and they procreate animals; and finally there are human beings, bringing forth human beings; all bringing forth according to their kind. *We have all experienced it that way; no one has ever experienced it any differently!* Not even Moses.

Talk about "thought, observation, and experiment." This is the real and basic creational truth of things. And we can trust it to be so! That way is now designated the way in which it was and came to be in the beginning, for all we can ever know. That scheme and story is what is first, real, and basic; all other stories are shots in the dark. This Genesis story comes to us with God's own Good-Housekeeping seal of approval. The world as we experience it is real, reliable, and radically foundational.

Any speculation about what was the case *before* the relatively full life world is resisted by the author of Genesis; it is cut off at the pass. Moses knows how to let God be God. He has no desire to figure out *how* God did it and where it all came from and how it came to be, other than out of God's own creative Word. The real-world results are naturally there for study and investigation, thank God. Moses is polite enough to know that he cannot discover any single key to it other than God and his Word. He doesn't look for some continuous equation or formula that will explain it all to us, that will justify our resistance to not-knowing. Who are we anyway to do that kind of stuff to God? Remember Job? Moses, by contrast, is ready to receive the world as he experiences and describes it in the text of Genesis as the word, witness, and testimony of the only One who was there. Anyone who goes there, beyond the world as given, and beyond what the text as witness gives, does not really end up with more than his/her own story, or myth. Among these myths one is as good as the next, for all we can ever know. There is the biblical realistic narrative with its inherent truth claims and there are all the others with their equally storied claims to be on to the truth of the matter. Truth claims inhabit all genres of literature: history, fiction, religious texts, science, poetry, and all the others.

The reader who sticks to the text as we have it may of course go so far as to claim that the text's claims and representations are not true. In that instance we are talking about the reader's response to the text, beginning with what is in the text and what claims it is putting forth. Disagreement as to whether those claims are true or not is perfectly possible from the human point of view. That is also the case about the world as described in the text of Gen 1:1—2:4b.

Separate Structures and Biblical Directives

There exist numerous parallel and putative "revelations." Through the successive epochs of civilization projections have varied. There were the ancient poetic and phantasmagoric versions, like that of the Zoroastrians. Then there were the speculations of the first age of reason, urged on by the anti-mythological speculations of Socrates, Plato, and Aristotle. In the Christian era also there emerged speculative ruminations about the intra-trinitarian life of God that eventually filled volumes of theological discourse, probably also because of the idea of objective reason present in medieval Scholasticism and in the new Enlightenment. Now in the modern era we have a more disenchanted, rarefied, elementary, narrowed down and seemingly controlled modern "scientific" rendering. It is no exception to the pattern of "religions" or "myths."

Numerous scholars have described the religious nature of those myths. Mary Midgley does so in her *Evolution as a Religion*. Vine Deloria Jr. argues this as well in his *Evolution, Creationism, and Other Modern Myths*. That said, everyone must acknowledge development, change, and differentiation in the processive sense. Herman Dooyeweerd, former professor of jurisprudence at the Free University of Amsterdam, always spoke, as a good Calvinist trained in law much as John Calvin himself had been, of the "creation law order" being descriptive of what God *established* and laid down in the beginning with his creative Word. For Dooyeweerd every word that comes out of the mouth of God is simply by virtue of that fact "law" word. God has structured a law-karma into the universe; to live and die happily, we must trust and "obey," because there's no other way. Once God established that creation law order in the beginning, there came to be development, unfolding, and the emergence of many things, but, of course, always *within* the context of the so-called "orders of creation." We shall discuss this way of construing original creation later when we discuss Karl Barth and the "Eclipse of Creation" in Protestant theology.

CHAPTER 9

Sin and the Fall

A. SIN AS PERVERSION

The complex "change" brought about by sin in the world, coming from the creatures of God and their willful transgressions, cannot be forgotten. As it unfolded, God's original creation was cared for (preservation or providence), especially following the enactment of the cultural mandate "to be fruitful and to multiply and replenish the earth." The "misdirection" of all things also became possible. This misdirection (per-version) did not generate anything *new* structurally or normatively, but it did take what was and "pervert" it, turned it around, abused and misused it. Sin turns good things away from God; restoration turns them back around again as it "converts" them.

For our purposes here this is a valuable distinction since it indicates that in every area of life things are directed to the service of God or misdirected to the service of something else and intra-mundane. This matter of direction distinguishes false religion from true religion. "Out of the heart are the issues of life" (Prov 4:23) is a favorite biblical citation of neo-Calvinists. There is a push in all things toward God or toward some substitute. For all Christian believers life is an unfortunate mixture of these two spiritive drives.

B. PARADISE

The Genesis creation narrative undoubtedly lays a claim to an original state of rectitude. Whether one accepts this to be the case or not is another matter. To put it in terms of John Milton's epic poem, there was a Paradise Lost. Good and evil are not two sides of the same coin. How evil came about we cannot know. Once again epistemically we are up against a brick wall with respect to this matter. It cannot be explained adequately by the powers of reason alone: looking for causes humans can only think back and back and back. However far back they go, there was always the problem of evil in everyone's life. To think only "naturally" about this gets one to the point of considering the two, good and evil, as coterminous. This is the stance taken in Zoroastrianism, Manicheanism, and Gnosticism. In the modern period it appears in evolutionism.

The text of Genesis challenges our "natural reason." Everything created is declared as "very good," and the text of Gen 1 says this so repeatedly that it simply cannot be missed. It is stressed more than any other characteristic of the original created order: *that it was very good*! Regardless of whether the hearer or the reader of the text accepts this to be the case, there can be no doubt that the narrative of Gen 1 *claims* this much as true. God is not responsible for sin; he is *not* the agent. Rather God's creatures, human and angelic, are the agents of it (Gen 2:4b—3:24).

Humans are responsible earthlings. As far as we can possibly know about the mystery of sin and evil, it is a *willful* creaturely transgression. Sin is not God divided against himself. It is not an inherent part of the created order, standing equally alongside the good. This is all we can say on the basis of the narrative; this is as far as we can go. We cannot fully know what the answer is to this distressing cosmic problem, and thus we must live with the not-knowing.

C. PARADISE LOST

Naturally Moses knew all about the reality of sin and evil, both personally and from his ancestors. Nonetheless the witness to an original state of right relationship with God was part of the *toledoth*, the witness of the generations. In projecting the Genesis saga back all the way to the beginning, Moses knew full well to include the insidious disruption of the fall. Despite this, Moses also firmly believed that God himself is very good, a goodness reflected in the product of the divine establishment of the created order (Gen 1:1—2:4b). Genesis 2:4b—3:24 is not a *second* story about creation, as is so often claimed by biblical historical critics, although it is fair to say that it is being claimed less so currently than it was twenty-five years ago. Moses reserved an additional chapter in Genesis to elaborate on the story of creation *and the fall* to designate the responsibility for evil to the willful transgression of God's creatures, both the human and the heavenly.

In these writings of Moses there is no inclusion of the ancient and modern views that good and evil are coterminus; that there is something good about evil. In the ancient world the Manicheans resorted to dualism of this sort in their conception of the divine. The later Gnostics too viewed our creational abode as something to be temporarily endured, while humans longed for flight from creation, for the "soul" to go to heaven when we die. The language used for this Gnostic view of the flight to heaven followed Plato's notion of the "noetic cosmos." Let us remember, however, that Plato was a Greek pagan, not a Hebrew. Plato's heritage was not the heritage of Joshua of Nazareth.

Modern thinkers have delved deep into this assertion that good and evil are coterminous. In *After the Apple*, Naomi Harris Rosenblatt ruminates on the idea that we would have missed a lot if Eve had not eaten the apple.[1] The same goes for Steve Jobs who founded Apple with the symbol of an apple with a bite out of it. Was he claiming that the bitten apple represents an applaudable advance of knowledge? Along these same lines modern evolutionism views the dark side of matters as the driving force of nature and history.

To keep things changing, there must be affirmation and negation, attraction and repulsion, expansion and contraction. These principles work together to give us not a piece of reality but the whole of it. The creative interplay of good and evil is a theme also frequently taken up in literature. Elizabeth Gilbert, in her novel *City of Girls*, entertainingly narrates the promiscuity of Vivian, the lively main character. Sex with many men other than the one Vivian really loves and with whom she has never had sex "satisfies the darkness" within her. For Gilbert, Vivian has experienced *all* of reality in this way, and thus makes her life "complete." Life would be too boring for Vivian without the darkness too.[2] In *City of Girls* the setting

---

1. Rosenblatt, *After the Apple*.
2. Gilbert, *City of Girls*.

is the 1960s, way ahead of the real sexual revolutions of later decades. Right or wrong, clearly this is *not* the view of Moses according to Gen 1–3.

D. THE FIRST PARADISE IS YET TO COME

The intractable question of where or how evil originated has also occupied Christian theologians. The influential neo-orthodox view developed by Karl Barth is one of the best known of such views. He suggests that from way before the foundations of the world, God chose to save. When God decides to do something, there's no stopping him. That's it.

However, God does need a platform on which to play out this real, predetermined drama. He needs an occasion whereby the great and eternal decision can be enabled or worked out. This *occasion* is logically implicit in the act of creation itself, because God's affirmation of creation implies dialectically, according to Barth, the threat of its negation, the primordial "chaos" power: "When God in the beginning created the heavens and the earth, the earth was a chaos" according to Barth's reading of Gen 1:1.

Moreover, the salvational plan of fulfillment among humans cannot be withstood by humans; all humans are swept up in this glorious plan of universal salvation, like it or not. The inevitable logic of Barth's thinking is worked out almost exclusively in terms of one person of the Trinity. One might refer again to this as Christocratic Unitarianism, theism that is exclusively Christ-centered. Thus too creation is partly negative right from the start so that the need for salvation is implicit in it. According to Barth's view, we should look for salvational encounters in the record book right from the start. Above all we shouldn't look back.

The Swedish theologian Gustaf Wingren called significant attention to the "Eclipse of Creation" decades ago when he published a book with that title. Wingren identified Karl Barth as the father of this eclipse of creation in modern theology, and I shall deal with that matter more extensively in chapter 10. For our discussion here it is necessary briefly to be reminded of some influences that predated Barth in the history of Western Christian thought.

In chapter 1 the Catholic Church's reduction of creation and revelation to natural law and natural theology was already introduced in our discussion. Also the Enlightenment's reduction of normative truth to science was mentioned in that chapter. In each of these ways the need for a Christian view of nature (or a theology of nature, if you will) was being discarded.

Finally added to that was Kant's attempt to retrieve a small bit of religion's relevance by granting it a socially therapeutic place in human life in the form of "values."

With those historical precursors in mind, what is immediately striking about Karl Barth's theological view as developed in his *Church Dogmatics* is his concentration on what he calls "the reality of nothingness." This discussion in Barth is designed to shed light on the "first" verse's assertion that "the earth was without form and void, and darkness was upon the face of the deep." Contrary to over twenty-four centuries of mainstream reading that has continued well into the twentieth century, Barth transforms the actual first verse of Gen 1, "In the beginning God created the heavens and the earth," into a *circumstantial clause* so that it reads "When in the beginning . . . ."

By heading up the first verse in this way, Barth intends to claim that the "waste and void," the nothingness that threatens, belongs to the dark side of God himself. It is the "non-essentiality" that God consciously passed by in his creation of the world. In fact, the reason for, or ground of, its being is God's refusal to will or affirm it. "Nothingness" is the uncreated possibility that exists because God chooses to act in creation. In the first act of God outside of himself, God separated the negative being from the elected and salvific work of his hands, as darkness from light. To light belong the acts of God in eternal election, and creation is really only the platform needed on which to execute election and temporal reconciliation. To darkness and the left hand of God belong wrath, judgment, and reprobation. Because God has from all eternity elected to save, nobody has anything to worry about (with the possible exception of Adolf Hitler).

Quite naturally then for Barth, already in the beginning creation is ambiguous with respect to God. What God chooses to affirm stands in need of continued support lest it be overwhelmed by the chaos power and nonbeing. The "very good" creation of God *ab initio* stands specifically in need of protection (salvation) against the dangers that threaten it. According to Barth this is the situation long "before" the fall of Adam and Eve into "sin." It is then in this way that Barth views the story of creation under the aspect of protection and safety, i.e., under the Christocentric model of saving responsiveness.

The nothingness is an enemy to be overcome, a challenge demanding response. Thus the Creator is essentially victor over the forces of darkness. God struggles with the threat of the primordial chaos and in the act of creation overcomes it. Accordingly, salvation can be viewed by Barth as rooted in the mind of God from long ago and then subsequently in the act of creation itself.³ Chaos possesses a power in existence prior to the fall and shows itself even at the creation of the world itself. As illustrative of this widespread acceptance in modern theology of the position that creation is a universal generated out of the experience of saving-responsiveness in salvation history, I would mention the following theologians: Gerhard von Rad, Bernhard Anderson, and Norman Young.⁴

Adding yet another dimension to the problem of viewing creation only as a divine act of saving responsiveness, the modern biblical theologian Claus Westermann has rightly and with considerable originality come down squarely on this issue in his book *Creation*. Calling attention to the "all-conquering scientific explanation of the origin of the world and of man" as presented by modern natural science since the Enlightenment, Westermann remarks that the church adopted a defensive position that "the Creation accounts in the Bible had nothing at all to do with scientific knowledge: they dealt with only religion and belief; the discussion was concerned with salvation."⁵

This restriction of the relevance of scriptural revelation to salvation, and of salvation to a putative "religious" dimension of existence, is concretely exemplified, according to Westermann, by the growing concentration of modern theology on the human being, specifically on man's understanding of himself in his present situation. But, writes Westermann, "when the theology and preaching of the church are concerned only with salvation, when God's dealing with man is limited to the forgiveness of sins or to justification, the necessary consequence is that it is only in this context that man has to deal with God and God with man." Westermann continues,

> This means that God is not concerned with a worm being trodden to the earth or with the appearance of a new star in the Milky Way. And so the question must be put: what sort of God is he who does everything for the salvation of man but clearly has nothing at all to do with man in his life situation? What can be the meaning of salvation history which has nothing at all to do with real history? Science has now stepped in as lord of the domain which man used to refer to [as] Creation What remains for God? This is the reason

---

3. Barth, *Church Dogmatics* 3/2:289–349.

4. Von Rad, "Theological Problem," 131–35; Anderson, *Creation Versus Chaos*, 49–55; Young, *Creation, Creator, and Faith*, 27–38.

5. Westermann, *Creation*, 2–4.

why some say "God is dead" and why many more say "The word God has no longer any meaning for me." And so it is an illusion to try to modernize a soteriology which has been cut off from reality and to update it in modern jargon. This is of no help. The matter stands or falls with the question, is God concerned with the real world which surrounds us? Is he Creator or not.[6]

My own formulation of the deficiency of a purely salvation centered theology might be slightly different. In his book called *The Theology of Nature*, George Hendry, my professor of systematic theology at Princeton Seminary, called it a "Christological constriction [that] came as near as any to being a unitarianism of the second article."[7] In any case modern theology's exclusive recourse to soteriological themes must be opposed. This bad move presupposes the assumption that the problem of the nature of the world as such falls outside of the scope of those things for the proper knowledge of which biblical revelation and the biblical creation story are necessary.

The problem of an account of nature is falsely consigned solely to the competence of an allegedly autonomous natural philosophy and science. Hardly any philosophers of science any longer consider science as a simple mirror of nature, or a simple reflection of what's out there. It is the reduction of the scope of revelation first to mankind, then to mankind's subjectivity, and finally to a putative "religious" dimension of consciousness that is objectionable. We have gone here from the illusions of an old, literalist orthodoxy to the equally absurd restrictions on religious beliefs of a new modernism. It is in this way, through a long, secularizing history, that the ground has been bulldozed out from under the narrative revelation about creation in Scripture.

As significantly, this restriction has forced religion to become identified with salvation whether in its rather highbrow European and Barthian version or in its more lowbrow American fundamentalist and evangelical strain. Finally, there has also attended this movement from illusion to restriction the devastating consequence of enslaving religion to alien and allegedly neutral but in effect secular analyses. This has undermined and dissembled the very concepts of embodiment that are required to make concrete and relevant sense of religion's own claims. Squarely against this modern assumption and its narrowing consequences, which represent the

6. Westermann, *Creation*, 2–4.
7. Hendry, *Theology of Nature*, 25.

Sin and the Fall

fateful bequeathal to theology of the deliverances of all-conquering secular philosophies, must be placed the Christian teaching and biblical narrative of creation with its philosophically relevant assumption that the light of the world emanates in no respect whatsoever from within the world itself.

The more we leave behind *creatio ex nihilo* by trimming it down to *creatio continua*, the more tolerable creation becomes for both many secular and Christian thinkers. There may never have been a first perfect creation, a Paradise Lost. Maybe Paradise is what is coming. Let's hope so. After all the outside pressures mentioned above, modern theology can possibly eke out a bit of what's left, but only down the line, of course. Maybe at the end of history. If there has never been a first perfect creation, then we should stop looking backward and instead look ahead. Is there really, when all is demythologized, a difference between a mythological Paradise Lost and keeping our fingers crossed for the life to come?

Before moving on to further discuss the eclipse of creation, it is useful to preface the way by including a few words about contemporary modern theologies that continue to advance the dramatic departure from creation orientation. Jürgen Moltmann, just recently passed away, wrote a book entitled *The Future of Creation*.[8] I got a copy, eagerly expecting some new and revised work on creation from a leader in the Barthian tradition. Lo and behold, the crucial words in the title turn out to be "the future."

Few works of contemporary theology marginalize creation thought more thoroughly than Moltmann's, with his almost exclusive focus on eschatology. Only in essay 8 in this collection does Moltmann mention creation, and then only to view the Christian misuse of the cultural mandate of Gen 1, coupled with modern science, as the cause of the ecological crisis. For Moltmann the gross error on the Christian side was the assertion that salvation history is the restoration of creation.[9] In its place he wants to put an urgently needed revision of the idea of creation that only can be acquired from current historical critical exegesis of the Younger Testament. "Biblically," Moltmann says, "faith in salvation as a historical process determines belief in creation; and in so far as redemption determines faith in salvation as a historical process, eschatology also determines the experience of history and belief in creation."[10]

---

8. Moltmann, *Future of Creation*.
9. Moltmann, *Future of Creation*, 116.
10. Moltmann, *Future of Creation*, 117.

CHAPTER 10

The Eclipse of Creation

A. KARL BARTH AND THE GERMAN CHURCH STRUGGLE

Gustaf Wingren, the chief critic of Anders Nygren's agape theology in the school of theology at the University of Lund in Sweden, identified not Nygren but Karl Barth as the dean of prejudice against the theology of creation in modern thought. As seen in the previous chapters, the modern story of the eclipse of creation cannot be told without reference to many pre-Barthian minimizations of a full biblical view of creation. However, in the twentieth century Barth's interpretation of Gen 1 became a focus of the debate. This is so because for Barth the story of creation in Gen 1 is the first location in the Bible of the overall biblical theme of salvation.[1] However another equally important factor in the Barthian story is his thought by association linking natural theology with National Socialist ideology. No adequate account of the plight of creation in modern theology can be given without consideration of the so-called German Church Struggle or "Kirchenkampf." Gustaf Wingren gives this account based on his own personal experience:

> I was confronted with the phenomenon of Barthianism after the war. I met Barth in person in many conferences before Evanston. I also met with the famous inter-national seminar at Basel during my stay there as a fill-in for Barth. In addition, during my stay as visiting professor at the University of Göttingen, I met with Barth's

---

1. See reference to this material on pp. 59–60 and on pp. 91–94 above. George Hendry calls Barth's volume 3 on creation in his *Church Dogmatics*, "certainly the weakest." Hendry, *Theology of Nature*, 25.

The Eclipse of Creation

two most famous German interpreters, Ernst Wolf and Hans Iwand. These meetings were all quite foundational, hard-hitting and lengthy, and in all three contexts the charge leveled against the doctrine of creation was the same: namely that it was the basis for varying forms of National Socialist theology.[2]

The three main ingredients in this story are the quasi-religious ideology of German National Socialism, the doctrine of the so-called creation ordinances (*Schöpfungsordnungen*), and the Christomonistic theology of Karl Barth. As stated so directly in Wingren's recollections, the immediate reasons why the doctrine of creation became so unpopular are not difficult to discern in this context.

Most histories of German thought and culture emphasize the political and economic roots of Nazi society and the Nazi state. What is not as often stressed is the quasi-religious background to National Socialism. Many Germans believed that the depression of Germany after WWI was symptomatic of a general cultural crisis. The breakdown of certainty in Germany was undergirded by a spiritual malaise of superhuman proportions. This malaise, it was thought, was based upon a sinful departure from principles that had from the beginning been built into creation. The chief manifestation of this departure from creation was intermarriage among the races. What God had put asunder Europeans had begun to unite. A homogenizing process threatened to weaken the superior racial groups responsible for the unparalleled achievement of Germanic culture in the nineteenth century. Though a superhuman genius would be required to bring about change, the process of deterioration had to be reversed because the original order of creation had to be restored.

Especially urgent would be "the final solution of the Jewish problem." However, German leaders anticipated considerable national as well as international reaction to the proposed solution and its immediate execution. In this preliminary stage of the revitalization program, there would have to be reindustrialization and remilitarization leading up to an unavoidable defensive war. Once these obstacles had been overcome, it was believed, a glorious millennium of peace and order, "*ein Tausend Jahre Reich*" would be ushered in.

Already in the 1930s within the church in Germany, the urgent question became how Christians would respond to this vision of swift practical, political, and institutional implementation. Many, some say the vast

---

2. Wingren, "Den Springande Punkten," 101. Tr. H. vd. Goot.

majority, of leaders and citizens advocated neutrality and a time for consideration during which, it was hoped, the more extravagant aspects of the Nazi program would be moderated. However, some smaller blocs within the German churches were ready for engagement. In the context of this political-theological controversy between Christian supporters and Christian opponents of the German cultural revolution under Hitler, vehement charges were hurled at the theology of creation. The theology of creation has continued to be a focal point for disagreement ever since, disagreement that continues to the present.

In the 1930s the theology of creation came to be increasingly identified in Germany with the so-called *Schöpfungsordnungen* and *Volksnomoslehre* of the Christian supporters of German National Socialism, a group within the church called the "*Deutsche Christen*." It was around this set of beliefs and the associated political sentiments of its adherents, who favored the Hitlerist revolution, that the German Church Struggle was fought. The modern history of creation faith is unintelligible apart from this chapter in the history of the German church.

Ecclesiastical and Christian opposition to the Nazis and their supporters in the church was spearheaded by Karl Barth. It was Barth and others associated with him in the so-called *Bekennende Kirche* or "Confessing Church" who issued a credal statement at Barmen in 1934. Their statement summarily rejected the naturalist and nationalist point of view of those within the church of Germany who were supporters of Nazism. The Barmen Confession in its first article states: "We reject the false teaching that the church can and must recognize any other events, powers, personalities, and truths apart from and in addition to this one Word of God as sources of its proclamation."[3] Because of the intense ideological turmoil of this period in the German church, the question of the doctrine of creation (creation orders and natural revelation) became much more than a specifically theological concern. It was taken up as a heated political issue as well. In all sorts of discussions, the question of natural theology and the Christian notion of orders associated with the doctrine of creation very quickly brought to the surface the question of political allegiance.

For Karl Barth in particular, whose radically kerygmatic and Christocentric theology undercut the basis of the doctrine of creation, this connection with the political situation was put to the test in a famous debate over natural theology in which he took up the case against Emil Brunner in

---

3. Cochrane, *Church's Confession Under Hitler*, 237-42.

1934. Along similar lines Barth debated the law-gospel question with Werner Elert in 1934 and 1935. Brunner and Elert each accepted some version of natural revelation. For Barth, however, this was exactly the fundamental error of nineteenth-century "culture Protestantism" that led straight from Schleiermacher to Hitler. Barth says,

> The error which has broken out today in the theology and Church politics of the German-Christians originated neither in the school of Luther nor Calvin, but is rather (Schleiermacher, R. Rothe, W. Beyschlag might be named . . . its particular fathers) the typical error of the final phase of that "Union" of the nineteenth century . . . . I can see absolutely nothing other in the German Christians than the last, most complete, and worst product of this modern Protestantism.[4]

For Barth the essence of the error of modern Protestantism was its acceptance of revelation through feeling, insight, and religious experience shaped by the present historical moment. He feared that such a revelation outside of the actual occurrence of it in Jesus Christ would come to predetermine the gospel, and thus it would prevent the Word of God from entering radically into human life. Any such framing of the Gospel might tailor it to present interests and the demands of the moment. Says Barth:

> If in the one holy catholic Church anything has to be relegated "to silence," it is the free private opinion (be it that of one individual or of countless people), which would make us seek and honour God as "Lord of history" today here and tomorrow there, this man in this way and that man in that. The Church is there, and only there, where God is sought and where He wants to be sought, but that means along with the witnesses, in the remembrance, investigation, exposition and application of that message of the Old and New Testament which alone established the Church and which alone can uphold it and will and shall continually renew it quite alone . . . . The Church, the German evangelical Church no less, lives on the one Word of God, from which she is born, and on no second word alongside it. This it is which must be opposed to the . . . German Christians.[5]

For Barth natural theology leads directly to National Socialism. His followers similarly associated theological questions and political concerns.

---

4. Barth, *German Church Conflict*, 27.
5. Barth, *German Church Conflict*, 32–35.

It often became the basis on which entire arguments were built. Wolfgang Tilgner's *Volksnomostheologies und Schöpfungsglaube: Ein Beitrag zur Geschichte des Kirchenkampfes* can serve as a good example for our purposes.[6] Tilgner dismisses Barth's theological critics on the basis of certain obviously reprehensible political propensities that he identifies in them. When dealing with a particularly complex relationship, Tilgner uses language that reveals his procedure of indictment by association. Having briefly sketched the so-called anti-Barmen theology of Werner Elert, especially in connection with the question of the *"natürliche Offenbarungsgesetz"* ("the natural law idea of general revelation"), Tilgner remarks, "With this . . . Elert lands in the neighborhood of the Volksnomos teaching of Stapel, even though he has not said directly that he has taken this position."[7]

Tilgner, furthermore, leaves the reader no doubt about his enthusiasm for the Barthian theology. Armed with an arsenal of Barthian absolutes ("the mistaken idea of natural theology," and "the unity of law and gospel"), Tilgner puts Barth's theological critics and ecclesiastical opponents to the test. We need only take the case of Paul Althaus to illustrate the rather predictable result:

> In connecting with the national-racial question in theology, the notion of primal revelation is to be judged critically. In the case of Althaus it is not clear whether this primal revelation is in every instance to be subordinated to the *post Christum* or whether in this idea there is a tendency to accept an independent historical basis for the knowledge of God. To be sure, in retrospect to the political theology of the 1930s, it must be said clearly that the creation ordinances can be put in proper perspective only from the center of the revelation of God in Jesus Christ. An independent natural theology is thus to be rejected. Only where the Gospel is taken seriously—which is often the hidden . . . inclination of Althaus—will the world and its orders be known for what they are: constantly broken and renewed limitations that God, out of his mercy and goodness in creation, uses for the proclamation of his saving grace.[8]

As an advocate of the idea of a "self-revelation of God in man and the world prior to and outside of Christ," Althaus is viewed through the single

---

6. Tilgner, *Volksnomostheologies und Schöpfungsglaube*, 210. Tr. H. vd. Goot.

7. Tilgner, *Volksnomostheologies und Schöpfungsglaube*, 210. Tr. H. vd. Goot. Wilhelm Stapel was a famous German nationalist and racist journalist.

8. Tilgner, *Volksnomostheologies und Schöpfungsglaube*, 200–201. Tr. H. vd. Goot.

The Eclipse of Creation

lens of the virus of natural theology; which, according to the witness of Barth, brought forth the German Christian support of Nazism, "the last, most complete, and worst product of . . . modern Protestantism."[9] There is little appreciation here for the fact that Althaus's theological problems are clearly not those of Barth and that Althaus's theory of a "self-revelation of God in the world prior to and outside of Christ" might be the expression of an important and legitimate insight. It appears that Tilgner is giving in to *argumentum ad hominem*.

These examples exemplify a more general phenomenon. Barth and his supporters were quick to see the faith issues at stake in the above-mentioned debates, as well as discussions surrounding Barmen, mainly in political terms. They did not take the religious position of their ecclesiastical and political opponents seriously. All too often the theological discussion became little more than evidence of the antagonism between Barth and his critics on the admittedly crucial matter of support or resistance to the Nazis. Accordingly, it cut off further consideration and constructive development of the truth of creation orientation, associated wrongly with the virus of natural theology that allegedly had led Germany straight from Schleiermacher to Hitler. In passing it is interesting to note that during the same time period in the 1930s and 1940s no such reaction occurred in the Netherlands against the rise of the Reformed, Christian "philosophy of the law idea," based as it was on a deeply rooted concept of creation ordinances. The Reformed Church in the Netherlands was not being faced politically with Nazism.

It is important to say at this juncture that in the crisis in Germany between 1930 and 1945 action was required; Barth and his associates surely acted with commendable moral indignation against the Nazi outrage. Nonetheless, it also should not be overlooked that Barth's polemic against natural theology and his corresponding turn to Christology were in part offered as alternatives to a false doctrine of creation being formulated by the politicized German Christians. The theology of Karl Barth cannot be treated in the abstract, because the main lines of Barth's argument were hammered out in the heat of battle. We are left with a crucial question. Can the main lines of his position be validly generalized and applied to situations for which the contexts are now dramatically different?

To answer this question we might need to consider whether a more appropriate Christian response could have been formulated in opposition

9. Tilgner, *Volksnomostheologies und Schöpfungsglaube*, 201.

to the Nazis. Maybe it would have been more to the point to have challenged the Nazis without first turning National Socialism into an alternative church and thus a theological heresy. Maybe it would have been more to the point to have challenged the Nazis on *political* grounds from a Christian point of view. Of course Barth acted. For this he must be acknowledged. But does that assure that he did not introduce theological distortions in his effort to do the right thing? For our present day thinking, could a better coordination of Christian faith and the political order be achieved? I continue to be puzzled that both Barth and the German Christians opted for varying forms of *Socialism* and the idea of the imperial state. How different might their conclusions have been if they had held firm to the answers that represent only *one* limited center of identity in human society and avoided the age long tendency to give away, in terms of rulership, what is God's alone? The mistake of political imperialism goes all the way back to Caesar and is almost as old as the ages.

After World War II, and thus after the collapse of National Socialism, the German Church Struggle was decided in Barth's favor. This fact for many entails a corresponding vindication of his theological position. As John Conway has noted in his book on the Church Struggle, those who told the story of the Confessing Church,

> were so imbued with the ideas of Karl Barth that they sought to direct the new thinking of the Church into Barthian channels. The history of the Church Struggle was therefore a vehicle for proving the validity of their theological viewpoints. Indeed, as one or two historians were constrained to point out, the Church Struggle was not primarily, as all the English-speaking writers assumed, the struggle between Church and State, but rather between rival theological parties within the Church. In their view it was a conflict between the true and the false Church and therefore of more consequent significance to the life of the Church long after the political persecutions of the Nazis had been forgotten.[10]

The conclusion of the Church Struggle represented a political settlement of a specifically theological issue. The theology of creation was identified as National Socialist, and theological attempts to work positively with the doctrine of creation have continued to remain suspect. Admitting the possibility of a revelation of God more original than and prior to the revelation of God the Redeemer in Jesus Christ is *not* yet admitting the possibility

---

10. Conway, *Nazi Persecution of the Churches*, xviii.

of an autonomous or natural knowledge of God in creation. Nonetheless, the attitude of Arnold T. Ehrhardt in a 1962 review of Gustaf Wingren's fine book on *Creation and Law* is not untypical:

> At this point I have to crave the forgiveness of my readers for not continuing beyond page 140 of Wingren's book; but the memories of so-called Lutheran productions which in the Nazi era misrepresented the Christian doctrine in a very similar fashion, produced by some of Wingren's German theological authorities, are still painfully vivid to my mind. Admitting then that there are a number of impressive passages and remarks throughout the book which would make me agree to the verdict that it is "excellent in parts," I nevertheless believe that theological literature is probably the last place to lay a curate's egg.[11]

With the collapse of National Socialism the death knell had also been sounded for the creation orders theologians. It is profoundly significant for the course of events in theology that the influence of these theologians, who were some of Barth's most competent and brilliant critics, was eclipsed after the war and that their names—such as Werner Elert, Emanuel Hirsch, and Paul Althaus in particular—have for all intents and purposes not been heard of since. This is certainly one of the tragedies of modern theology, and it is directly related to the fact that the *theological* issue of the doctrine of creation was essentially *politically* settled.

The compromise of creation faith, which is now receiving less attention than it deserves, in large measure explains the disregard and neglect of creation thought from the 1960s to the present. The neo-orthodox view has not only influenced German ecclesiastical affairs but also has had an impact on world ecclesiastical affairs as well with the dominance of Christological and eschatological theologies that have developed beyond, though out of, the basic framework of neo-orthodoxy. It is fair to say, I believe, that the direction of theology today cannot be adequately understood apart from the phenomenon we have sketched above, and which is called the "eclipse of creation." This phenomenon exposes the double catastrophe of Nazism: how both its supporters on the right and its opponents on the left were victimized by it.

---

11 Ehrhardt, "Christianity and Law," 310.

B. EVOLUTIONISM AS THE SECULAR ECLIPSE OF CREATION

The most strident source of the secular eclipse of creation in modern thought may be found in evolutionism. A compromise with evolutionism within Christianity is often called "theistic evolutionism," or "concordism." The latter two options are attempts to have it both ways. All of these positions fail at a proper understanding of the integration of faith and learning as well as of what the revelation in Gen 1:1—2:4b warrants as proper control beliefs about creation.

Biblical revelation funds each of the scientific disciplines comprehensively at its origin and thus in its operations with respect to its facts, models, judgments, and interpretations; this includes the discipline of theology. This is Christian orthodoxy's basic belief about revelation. The self and its judgment, or what the self imagines to be possible or impossible, cannot be the foundation of judgment in any context, natural science included. Thus to make the self a source of judgment is to challenge Christian orthodoxy with a modernist or secular option.

Moreover, the "modernist" and secular options are most likely to be chosen with respect to (1) a distinction between what in the biblical text is thought to be the central message and what is merely packaging and (2) what observation and the senses teach and what science has concluded from its observations augmented with computation and extrapolation.

By contrast to these notions about sources of truth, I would assert the holistic view that scriptural revelation ought to fund each of the sciences comprehensively at its origin. In book 1 of the *Institutes of the Christian Religion*, John Calvin speaks out against the Scholastics in particular. Only the Bible, he says, can teach us about original creation because in a broken world creation can no longer teach us about itself.[12]

Marvelously Calvin begins his religious discourse not with God but with the *knowledge* of God. After introducing his formal doctrine of Scripture, Calvin begins his discussion of the knowledge of God the Creator, acknowledging at the same time a knowledge of God as Redeemer "in Scripture," a knowledge *that will follow and that comes second*. It is clear, Calvin says, "that God has provided the assistance of the Word for the sake of all those to whom he has been pleased to give useful instruction because he foresaw that his likeness imprinted upon the most beautiful form of the

---

12. Calvin, *Institutes* 1.6.1–2; cf. also 1.2.1.

universe would be insufficiently effective."[13] The self-manifestation of God in creation remains but has become "ineffectual" because humans can no longer grasp it as they ought apart from the self-disclosing Word of God in Scripture.

Because God has put revelation and reason together in the same way for all persons, belief is basic for all. Science is, in fact, pre-theoretically funded by some taken for granted source, be it the true one or a substitute one that finds its absolute concern *within* the world. Though the Bible is a single canon, incidental truths occur in the text of the Bible that might be cognitively significant for science at its foundations. This is the case even though these "incidentals" are not themselves scientific in character. How appropriate it is to speak of "incidentals" in this regard is itself a good question, since the putative central message is presented in the text only through a complex and concrete setting.

In any event, from a constructive point of view we should ask how the text of Gen 1:1—2:4b might be viewed so as to highlight matters of basic pre-theoretical relevance to natural science, to the *meta*-physical roots of science. What vision of things do we have in the text that can and should effectively influence the scientific study of creation at its inception? Since the study of creation is not equivalent to science as such, but is to science's two forms (Bible-informed and Bible-uninformed), these questions are urgent.

Abraham Kuyper calls the original distinction between God and the not-god the "*moedertegenstelling*." In literal translation he is calling this distinction "the mother of all distinctions" or "primal differentiation." Everything else is "given birth" through this. To make the reader ever cognizant of this fundamental boundary-line, Kuyper suggests that "God thought it fitting to reflect that boundary line in the firm boundaries that he established among his creatures." In other words, Kuyper continues, "God anchored the separations among all between creation and himself."[14]

1. Creation and Time

From Gen 2:2–3 we learn that when God's work of the original creation was finished, which primarily involved acts of separation, God rested, having blessed and hallowed the seventh day. God's day of ceasing from his creative work signifies that his creative work of origination was truly finished,

13. Calvin, *Institutes* 1.6.3; also 1.6.4.
14. Kuyper, *Ijzer en Leem*, 11–12.

complete in principle. His work was an original act of establishment governed by *ex nihilo* creation (Gen 1:1—2:4b) and everything else happens after and thereupon.

On the one hand there is the calling of all things into existence, each after its own kind, the unique and mysterious action of creation about which we know only by revelation; and on the other hand there is a genetic process of unfolding and development within the orders and kinds after God ceases his original work. Nothing could be clearer in Gen 1 and 2 than that God's original creative act of establishment is unique. It is the completed foundation of all subsequent and ongoing unfolding. This includes the whole cosmic array of kinds from stones, plants, animals, and on to speaking human beings. Everything depends on how seriously we take this "in the beginning" of Gen 1, and it also depends on how seriously we take the claim that the divine action that governs what took place in this "time" of creation came to a definite end.

Like never before in Western thought the pressure is on to diminish this *creatio ex nihilo* as dramatically as possible. The eclipse of creation is evidence of this. That drive has reached its peak in the quest for a story of meta-physical evolutionism, or for what Mary Midgley has called *Evolution as aReligion*.[15] In a similar fashion Vine Deloria Jr. has dared to call this story "evolution as myth."[16] Many have come to pass by the significant plain sense of Gen 1:1—2:4b because another story has become the spectacles through which they, also many Christians, now read the Genesis story and through which they selectively and reductivistically view creation reality itself. There is a strong push to read the story in *concord* with what many believe is science.

In Gen 1:1—2:4b we are dealing with an absolutely unique, a once-for-all, transcendent action of creation whereby, in the mystery of God's movement outside of himself, the not-god and all that is contained in it, including time itself, became established and founded. The Dutch theologian Herman Bavinck speaks in this connection of creation as *"ontstaan,"* as having been originated, as well as now having *"bestaan,"* existence.[17] Moreover, epistemically speaking, this action and its result are *revealed* to us in Genesis, in Scripture. Natural reason in none of its forms can help us out here.

15. Midgley, *Evolution as a Religion*.
16. Deloria, *Evolution, Creationism, and Other Modern Myths*.
17. Bavinck, *Gereformeerde Dogmatiek*, 394.

The Eclipse of Creation

According to Gen 2:2–3, it can only be said of the original, transcendent, and unfathomably mysterious act of absolute creation that it is "complete," finished once and for all. Could the words of the Bible about this point have been any clearer or any more lucid? And yet in the discussion of Gen 1 and 2 many whisk on by them. As deeply pressured as we have become by continuing creation thinking (*creatio continua*), many run on to Gen 2:4b and following as if we had crossed no discontinuous boundary, as if continuity and uniformity were universal and absolute.

Please note, only about the original creation can it be said that it is complete and finished. This can never be said about what follows or happens subsequently in the order of space and the duration of time. Dutch philosopher Herman Dooyeweerd has stated it as follows:

> Even now the process of becoming continues constantly; individual men, animals, plants, etc. come into existence in bodily forms. This is no temporal continuation of God's work of creation, but rather a working-out in the temporal order of the completed creation. Even though an enormous period of time, in which the fundamental structures of the cosmos have been realized themselves in a process of successive cosmic evolution since then terminated, preceded the origination of individually created thing . . . within a cosmos already unfolded in its fundamental structures, this original process of cosmic evolution too was nothing other than the working out of the God completed work of creation within the temporal order. This original process thus only brings [out] God's established creation order . . . successively in a rich diversity of aspects and structures of individuality.[18]

What we are given "in the beginning," what is established by God, what has been laid down before the foundations, appears *with time*, not *in time*, though it is almost impossible to communicate this without using the categories of time. It is because the original creation transcends time itself that in the beginning human beings and the various types of animals and plants do not have their origin in other preexisting types. Their distinguishing differences are not due to modifications in successive evolutionary generations. The original creation is, for all anybody can ever know, not the product of gestation, or birth, which are the properties of becoming, but is the result of a fiat or a declaration. "Let there be, and there was." There is a significant logical distinction made in what the text says.

---

18. Dooyeweerd, "Schepping en Evolutie," 115. Tr. H. vd. Goot.

Creation as an Introduction to Christian Thought

The great chain of distinctions in Christian orthodoxy that begins with Creator and creation and includes the separation and division of creatures from one another culminates in the distinction between original creation, or establishment, on the one hand, and providence or governance of becoming on the other. In context after context the Bible represents a sustained polemic against blurring the boundaries: between God and the world, between humans and animals, between creation and providence, between clean and unclean, between Israel and Canaan, between creation and redemption, between special and common grace, and finally even between God and humanity in Jesus Christ, for even these are joined together *without confusion*.

There are two interesting contexts in which this theme of limits and boundaries and a corresponding biblical call to heed them appears: in the holiness and cleanliness codes of Leviticus and in the wisdom literature of Proverbs. According to Mary Douglas, holiness and cleanliness as set forth in Leviticus requires that "individuals shall conform to the class to which they belong.... Holiness means keeping distinct the categories of creation. It therefore involves correct definition, discrimination, and order." Douglas concludes, "Holiness is . . . a matter of separating that which should be separated."[19]

A second example can be taken from the book of Proverbs. Writing on "liminal thinking" in Prov 1–9, Old Testament scholar Raymond Van Leeuwen argues that the system of symbols of "paths," of the "strange" and good women, and "houses" represent sexual ethics. He describes it as "a particular instance of the general requirement that humans respond to the limits placed on them by creation" for "recognition of cosmic structure or limits is inseparable from proper eros or direction." Van Leeuwen concludes that "like other symbol systems in OT thought, Proverbs depicts the world as segmented by boundaries, by limits that apply in every person, thing, and function [cf. Gen 1]. Limits in the social sphere are grounded in and reflect the segmented order of creation itself."[20]

In the worldview of John Calvin we also see a prominent place given to the notion of boundaries, limits, separations, and antitheses.[21] This has been carried forward in the works of the two great reformers of nineteenth-century Calvinism in the Netherlands, Abraham Kuyper and Herman

---

19. Douglas, *Purity and Danger*, 53–54.
20. Van Leeuwen, "Liminality and Worldview," 10–11.
21. Bouwsma, *John Calvin*, 34–36.

The Eclipse of Creation

Bavinck. The separation-distinction motif is so striking that Abraham Kuyper ascribes to God the name *Hamabdil*, literally "the Separation Maker," in order appropriately to characterize his sovereignty as portrayed in the text of Genesis. Both Kuyper and Bavinck have been unrelenting in their attempts to apply this scheme of boundaries and creational limits and its biblical assumptions to every area of thought. In a previous segment I have taken special note of the prominence throughout the narrative of Gen 1 of the separation-division theme, and I have emphasized how this distinction has been made metaphysically irrelevant in evolutionism's philosophical scheme of things.

In *De Verflauwing der Grenzen*[22] Abraham Kuyper also develops a social theory that is a sustained polemic against all *unitary* concepts of the social order that seek to subordinate the differentiation of the social centers of initiative ("sphere sovereignty") to a single structural principle. The prime case in point of this blurring of the boundaries for Kuyper is modern socialism, the idea that everything belongs to Caesar or the state. Similarly, throughout his works Kuyper rejects in the natural domain the transformationist theory that regards all individuality and specificity as evolutionary products from an original homogeneity. His occasional concessions to the special theory of microevolution *within* the kinds as given in creation has been used by persons unfamiliar with the Kuyper corpus as a whole to detract from the overall force of what Kuyper is asserting. Unfortunately much of his work still appears only in Dutch.

Because of the difficulties posed in Gen 1 with the concept of "day" as clock time, as we have said in a previous chapter, already long ago Augustine suggested in his *The Literal Meaning of Genesis* that the notion of "day" actually seems to be used to specify the successive "topics" of creation.[23] Each day is like a new topic. Indeed, in a literal reading of the term "day" the order of the creatures also poses a challenge, as Leon Kass has argued, because "there is light in the absence of sun or any light-giving heavenly bodies; and there is terrestrial vegetation (Day 3) before the sun (Day 4). In short, though all the beings are familiar, the order of their appearance does not square perfectly with the facts of ordinary experience."[24] It was this kind

---

22. Amsterdam, 1892. A translation into English by J. Hendrik de Vries appeared in vol. 53 (1893) of the July and September issues of *The Methodist Review*, pp. 520–35 and 762–78.

23. Augustine, *Literal Meaning of Genesis*, 134–45.

24. Kass, "Evolution and the Bible," 31.

of realization and the biblical conviction that everything which is not-god is thereby "creature" that led Augustine also to argue that time was created *with* the world.[25] The divine act of original creation, which was completed only with the seventh day, did not itself take place *in time as ordinarily understood as duration*. It also did not take place in time as if time were a sort of container.

Of the divine works that God moved outward to do, creation out of nothing is absolutely unique, and therefore the story about it is also unique in the Bible. Nonetheless, the story is accommodated to the language and assumptions of an already completed creation order. The story tells the reader that there was the para-temporal act of original creation, and after "it was finished, God ceased from his original work." Only thereupon ensues a fully *temporal* process of unfolding and development *within* the "kinds" as established in the beginning. There is the absolutely trans-temporal execution of the decision or resolve to create. This I call the *mystery* of creation. There is also the "creating time" of Gen 1 that only bears analogy to the full temporality of the completed creation that we all now experience, and finally there is the full temporality of the created process of unfolding and becoming. There is no way to clarify the revelation concerning creation in the Bible without at least minimally using these or such like distinctions. In an article in *Dialogue*, theologian Gordon Spykman uses the term "time-in-the-making" to refer to the same thing that I have called "creating time," which is to be distinguished from historical time, or time-as-we-know it.[26]

In the early church and among the Reformers "days" are distinguished according to what is created in each of them.[27] Ultimately "day" is a distinction in time because it is first and foremost a distinction *in being and in kinds*. The two go together in the Bible. In the ancient Hebrew world, "day" and "time" indicate the rich variety and arrangement of behavior. "Day" and "time" represent the cosmic order of succession, that rich diversity of distinct and separate things successively ordered in relation to one another from the simplest physical realities of earth, water, and air to plants, animals, and on to human beings, culminating finally in the holiness of the Sabbath. Or as Leon Kass has put it: "the sequence of creatures [in Gen 1] may not be mainly or primarily an effort to tell a . . . temporal story. Rather, the apparently temporal order could be an image for the ontological order;

---

25. Augustine, *Literal Meaning of Genesis*, 153–54; cf. also *City of God*, bk. 1, 212.
26. Spykman, "Beginnings," 9.
27. Luther, *Lectures on Genesis*, 5.

the temporal sequence of comings-into-being could be a vivid means of conveying the *hierarchic* order of the beings-that-have-come-to-be-and-are." Concludes Kass, "We need a second, and different, kind of look at the biblical sequence."[28]

The work-a-day week with its seven-foldness is merged in the text of Gen 1 with a catalogue of the many topics that the author, Moses, treats as he describes the world as God created it and as Moses experienced it in his present moment of writing. He then projects it back on to the *beginning*. For Moses and the Bible this is as far "back" as any human can go without constructing an alternative or substitute myth. In this world, as it was constituted in the beginning by God, humans were made to live; from such a beginning humans hail; and finally, in a fallen world, unto an end properly developed according to the order established in the beginning they are destined to be redeemed and restored.

We might reconstruct the inspired biblical author's line of thought and action as follows. It is as if the author of Gen 1 has just stepped into the great theater of the universe and is describing its many features before beginning to describe the drama of covenant history. He takes special note of all the things that we experience daily and that daily surround us, and he views them as things of the house of creation within which the years of our lives run their course. This rich creation with its roughly experienced, and thus known, differences is what the author judges to be the real world. We know the difference between a human being and an animal when we see them. Everyone from the past has seen this too. For all anyone, including the natural scientist, can or will ever know, the author suggests by the mode of his portrayal, we have received it, and still receive it, from the hands of God *just as we experience it*.[29]

2. Creation Versus Evolutionism as Separation Blind

As we have seen, the biblical story of creation expresses a deep appreciation for the different degrees and grades of being-present that are manifest here on earth. Matter and living things are discontinuously, abruptly different; so too plants in comparison to animals; and finally so too animals as compared to human beings. We shall never be able to get beyond these basic, known, and experienced differences no matter what tools we use. Moreover,

---

28. Kass, "Evolution and the Bible," 32.
29. Vander Goot, *Interpreting the Bible*, 81–82.

the state of the modern, empirical natural sciences also most frequently confirms this reality, though many scientists still hope for discoveries in the links of the stream of nature that would confirm their transformationist beliefs as warranted.

There seems to be little conflict between the basic structure of the biblical picture of Gen 1 and the results of nonspeculative, modern, natural science. For the author of Gen 1 the phenomenally given world, the world as human beings have always experienced it with its roughly given differences of kinds is trustworthy. What we have now in its basic differentiations is what God gave us in the beginning, at the point of origin, *for all we can know*. The "days" of creation are still present with us. The separations that exist among things are real and basic, and thus, for all we can know, were there already in the beginning as the author of the text pictured that beginning for us. The world is not merely matter evolving, or mere matter governed by mere physical law, but a cosmic order of succession.

The author of Gen 1 assumes that we know the radical differences among things, stones, plants, animals, and human beings. And so this world as we experience it, the one in which we know its basic differentiations, is the only real world, and hence is the world as far back as we can trace it.

We might ask whether the desire to trace it back further into the mystery of creating time, or of the transcendent act of original creation, is not motivated by the desire of humans to blur the boundary between God and themselves. Are modern humans desirous to know how it was done so that they might "repeat" it out of the desire to prove that finally they too have creation under their control, that they too are really god?

The world as presented in the text of Gen 1 differs dramatically from the world as now modeled for us by the abstractive sciences undergirded by evolutionist, tranformationist reductionism. "Thought, observation, and experiment" have been augmented (replaced?) with "modeling," which involves having a hunch, looking for evidence that fits the hunch, and then putting it out there as "fact." Naturally humans can conceptualize the physical characteristics of the cosmos; scientists can construct an image or blueprint or computational model of the whole with reference only to physical essences or physical time. But that rarefied image is not the experience of diversity from which all of our thinking sets out and to which all of our responsible and abstractive thinking must return. Significantly, it is the world of everyday life with its multiplicity of forms and kinds that the scriptural text and its author present to us. The text's world is not the world

The Eclipse of Creation

as each science reduces it to a single essence, or law, or continuous material. The text's world is not like the world that evolutionistic theory arranges in a continuous temporal order of evolution from simple to complex, from dust and energy to human beings.

For the author of Gen 1 the absolute beginning, the first principle, is pluriform according to the narrative's structure of the seven-fold week. There are the different things and various kinds of laws governing them. If these distinguishable things did not exist in actuality in the beginning, then surely the various kinds and the qualitatively different kinds of laws governing them came into existence in principle. In the Latin Vulgate interestingly enough the phrase *in principio* is used as the proper translation of the first three words of the Bible "in the beginning," or *baraseth*. If the concrete entities themselves appeared only later in the temporal process of unfolding, then in the beginning they were all "made" beforehand as makeable and thus were present at least "potentially" in the world before they were deployed. This latter, fairly reasonable position is the view of Jon Lever, J. H. Diemer, and Herman Dooyeweerd.[30]

In any case, no "kind" that is in the beginning emerges on the scene through "evolution as transformation of the species," but rather each appears in the beginning as *distinct* already, as Adam and Eve clearly do in the story. To suggest otherwise in terms of the text's self-understanding would be "absurd."[31] Moreover, the principle of the unity of things is spiritual and resides in God himself. The theistic-evolutionist's conception of what is originally created seems strangely reductionist by insisting that only matter or dust and energy evolved strictly in accordance with physical law.

Contrary to this kind of evolutionism to which theism is sometimes simplistically accommodated, the Bible teaches, it seems to me, that creation is the idea of a cosmic order arranged according to the scheme of seven distinct "days" of things, all of which were created in the beginning out of nothing, whether in actuality (as I myself prefer to take it) or maybe just in principle. The different creatures are irreducibly distinct, and development thus takes place *within* the kinds or kingdoms (micro-evolution) as given in the beginning, not from one kind to another of a qualitatively

---

30. Lever, *Creation and Evolution*, 219–22. See also Diemer, *Nature and Miracle*, 2–6. And see Dooyeweerd, "Schepping en Evolutie," 116–18, where Dooyeweerd stresses again and again the difference between God's transtemporal work of creation and the creaturely result or product of it as this unfolds successively in the cosmic order of time.

31. Boer, "Arbitrary Nonsense," 3–4.

different sort (macro-evolutionism). The story of macro-evolutionism and the narrative of creation in Gen 1 seem incompatible.

Ideally the story of creation and the sciences of creation reality should not stand in tension with one another. However, much natural science in the modern period does stand in this tension because natural science, or any science for that matter, is not simply the mirror nature. Neither do they mirror general revelation, as understood by complementarists and concordists. So-called facts always appear in an antecedent framework. Creation reality must be carefully distinguished from the human grasp or interpretation of it in a fallen world such as we all inhibit. Indeed, especially after the Wars of Religion, many were propelled to see the emerging natural sciences as exempt from outside influences or human conditioning. Science and natural reason were credited with occupying an Archimedean point of universal objectivity. In the most current philosophies of science this assumption no longer holds, even though in mass media we still hear confident astonishment about persons "who do not *believe* in science."

Calvin describes well the fact that fallen human beings grasp the world amiss and often willfully misconstrue it according to their own likes and dislikes, thus rendering the revelation in creation "ineffectual."[32] This misconstrual of the world pervades the allegedly immune aspects of scientific thought. As Karl Barth has argued rightly and forcefully, far from complementing biblical revelation, the attempt to grasp the revelation in creation in itself apart from the Word reduces it to an alternative revelation in disguise.[33] How much differently might we not understand modern natural science by taking this tack?

Concordists or theistic evolutionists argue, by contrast, that no real conflict exists between scientific reason and biblical religion, because the former only deals with the "how" of creation whereas the latter deals with the "why." God is good enough to get brought in at the beginning and at the end of the creation project. As a result the intrinsic process of the "how" of creation is left to modern science to define. Once the definition of that internal process has been established by the majority in science, these theologians and scientists step in to call it God's strategy, or the mechanism God used to execute his creative activity. "Science says" has become intimidating for many.

---

32. Calvin, *Institutes* 1.1–1.5.
33. Barth, *Dogmatics in Outline*, 17, 20, 23, and 60–61.

The Eclipse of Creation

There seems to be a deeply ingrained tendency among research scientists and scholastic theologians to exempt science from contextual limitations that normally apply to human thinking. In universities today we hear much from the human and contextual disciplines about the personal and culturally conditioned character of human thought and its philosophic nonneutrality. Even an amateur in the area of the philosophy of science comes immediately upon the common claim that knowledge in the natural sciences also is personal and context dependent. Those who argue that science deals with the "how" of creation and Christian faith with the "why" create the impression that the natural sciences, if they put effort into it, can be protected from these limitations. Christian participants fostering this view reveal that the origin of their concept of reason is in their own Scholastic heritage, in which the idea of general revelation is translated into a derived view that both creation reality *and the ability to grasp it correctly* are given to human beings in general. This view is usually referred to as "natural revelation" or "natural theology."

This adoption of natural theology becomes a matter of special concern when theistic evolutionists advocate not simply evolution but transformism or macro-evolutionism as well. Macro-evolutionists attempt to explain the continuous processive development of the original, physical material of the cosmos governed by physical law and use that view as an alleged account for the appearance of the nonphysical as well. Most claim, as Darwin did 150 years ago, that the final, fully adequate explanation is yet to be found, but meanwhile they are confident that it will be in the near future. Much of what simple evolutionary theories have to say might be acceptable, if it were not for the fact that they are tied in dogmatically with macro-evolutionistic transformationism. In this shift there is a critical failure to account for the genuinely different degrees and distinct grades of being that are clearly present here on earth. The error lies in assuming that what comes "after" necessarily evolves "out of" what came before. Actually the accumulated scientific evidence itself casts doubt on this assumption.

It is worth noting that without the dogma of macro-evolutionistic transformationism, much of what the natural sciences have uncovered could be coordinated with Christian faith and the saga of creation in Scripture. The diversity of kinds is there, but the intrinsic linkage of all the kinds in an unobserved process of fourteen billion years of time is not there. This was acknowledged by the famous Roman materialist Lucretius, who lived before the birth of Jesus. As a strict materialist following Epicurius,

Lucretius "posited . . . what he called a 'swerve.' Lucretius' principal Latin word for it was 'clinamen,' an unexpected, un-predicatable movement of matter."[34]

Allow the Christian advocates of the biblical view of creation a few "swerves" when it is found that space cannot explain motion, that motion cannot explain the chemical, that combined chemicals are not enough to constitute life, that plants don't explain animals, and last but far from least, that animals did not bring forth human beings. Why believe defensively in a continuous stream of matter and energy when macro-evolutionists following the materialist Lucretius could accept a few "swerves" and have us all *roughly* on the same page, at least all of us in line with the evidence at hand?

One can only wonder why the tradition-laden and time-honored commitments of Christian thought must be modified, overhauled, or restricted to make room for the claims of modern natural science. From the point of view of Reformed Protestantism, it would be odd indeed that the claims of science as the *interpretation* of general revelation should be confused with general revelation itself.

I say "odd" because in the Reformed tradition the Bible and general revelation do not have equivalent epistemic status. The Bible has been given by God after the fall precisely to remedy the human grasp of general revelation, which grasp has, according to Calvin, become "ineffectual" in a fallen world. Apparently, then, even in spite of the fall, the Bible represents the possibility of a noetic clarity that general revelation could never bring about; unless, of course, one accepts the idea of "natural theology" or natural reason, as in the Scholastic traditions. What else would Reformed theology have in mind when ascribing "perspicacity" to the Bible but not to general revelation in a fallen creation?

In addition, as revelation the Bible represents already within itself the two-foldness of Word from on high and human responses or interpretations of it. These two together belong to the *one revelation of the Word of God in the Bible*. Among other things this means on the first order level that believing and loving responses to the Bible, which are always directed to the what-is-said-in-the-way-in-which-it-is-said, should not be demoted to the status of an "interpretation." This is all the more so if by "interpretation" is meant the relative and mediational interpretation achieved on a second order level, by those who make no claim of commitment to the text or

---

34. Greenblatt, *Swerve*, 7.

The Eclipse of Creation

being shaped by it. This presumed "neutrality" drives most historical and literary critical approaches to the text. In order to be taken seriously by the Christian, they would require that an act of faith (ac)knowledge(ment) has already taken place on the first order level of engagement with the text,[35] as would be the case in Christian philosophy or in any philosophy.[36]

One wonders further why the time-honored claims of Christian faith must be modified, or altered or restricted since the matters on which physics, especially astrophysics, pronounces are so far beyond all ordinary reach, so complex, and so shrouded in unfathomable mystery. As the Nobel Prize winner in physics Ilya Prigogine says, "present knowledge in astrophysics is still scanty and very problematic."[37] Contingent on an analysis of and extrapolation from a very limited set of physical variables, the cosmological claims of astrophysics appear speculative. How could a practitioner of that science who has searched it at the highest levels of expertise still raise such doubts if the claims of physics that are intrinsic to its domain are simply "factual," as value free as baking a cake or dialing a phone?

From theistic evolutionists and concordists one garners less than an accurate impression of the proper relationship between current evidence in the natural sciences on the one hand and frameworks or beliefs and theories on the other. There is of course the dominance of reputational credibility with regard to "science as facts" in the natural sciences, and it obscures the actual debates that occur within these disciplines. Dissenting voices are often excluded from the discussion. The majority of the participants, unable to detect the "motion" of the thought system because they are part of it, all stand together as a force powerful enough to discredit or even to ignore those who offer alternative construals of the data. The majority shuns the theoretical minorities and acts as if they do not deserve any real standing within the guild of the science.

It has become less and less clear what the evidence really is; a good case can be made for the claim that the real Achilles heel of theistic evolutionism is its empirically unwarranted and thus unscientific claims about the process of evolution. Theistic evolutionism attaches itself to a materialistic view of the original stuff of creation and to a hard and physical notion of law, to uncompromising continuity thinking, and thus to naturalistic transformationism, claiming that the apparently higher or more complex

---

35. Vander Goot, *Interpreting the Bible*, 1.
36. Wolterstorff, *Reason Within the Bounds*.
37. Prigogine and Stengers, *Order Out of Chaos*, 116.

comes *after* the lower and less complex, as well as out of it in many cases. These claims leave them vulnerable to the accusation of being inadequate science as well as unacceptable Christian theism. In the next section I will take up the matter of evidence and beliefs as this is being reconsidered in the philosophy of science. Following that section I will also consider the matter of dissenting voices within the natural sciences themselves.

3. Evidence and Theory in the Natural Sciences

Scientists are seldom making simple observations. Rather they are almost always engaged in a process of extending previous theories by guessing what the next step might be as it extends that theory. The evidence that the scientist gathers is collected for the purpose of substantiating a hypothesis which has been formulated *before* the gathering of evidence. Scientists do not simply go about observing everything available to them. They pursue lines of investigation that focus certain events while at the same time leaving others unattended. Good procedure requires selectivity.

The selection of evidence becomes especially important in any science using hardware or measuring instruments. The devices for gathering data are an extension of theory, and the construction of devices themselves is based on what the theory predicts. Because measuring devices are theory-based and because the evidence sought answers to the already formulated conjectures, the evidence of science is not plain for all to see. It is only plain for persons already part of the conversation who have agreed that the methods used are the most satisfactory way of testing the hypothesis.

There are features of the scientific enterprise that cast doubt on the claim of simple objectivity even in the most restricted sense. If by this claim of objectivity is understood that the conclusions of scientists are based on evidence and that evidence is clearly there for anyone to see, then this claim simply does not coincide with what actually happens as science is disseminated. Actually the naive notion of objectivity is part of the scientific lore that is presented to nonscientists when scientists dispense their conclusions. But it should be noted that scientists rarely make their actual evidence available to the consumers of their ideas, that is, to the public. What gets circulated is summaries and claims that scientists insist are justified by their privately held evidence. It is not uncommon for other scientists to question the methods as well as the interpretations if they have access to the evidence.

The Eclipse of Creation

This brings us full circle. Scientists need theoretical sophistication in order to know what to explore, and, once their explorations lead to evidence, they can only make sense of the evidence if they know the theories by which the search was generated in the first place. What is objective about that? Those of us who are the "consumers" of scientific pronouncements depend entirely on the word of experts. That sounds quite subjective to me.

Not only do nonscientists accept scientific knowledge in a subjective fashion, but scientists also do this among themselves. This is unavoidable because the largest portion of experts in a field must begin by accepting much in the field from other experts. This is what science education is about. There is an accumulated body of knowledge in a field, and it is taught to students who gradually as they become more skilled are allowed to join into some of the activities of the scientific guild. A scientific researcher knows only a fraction of that accumulated body of knowledge by having gone through the actual evidence and using it to test the widely accepted theoretical conjectures that constitute the accepted body of knowledge in that field. Most of what the scientists know is based on other scientists' evidence and interpretations.

Even in the case of direct work being done with the "evidence" in the sciences, the stance of the so-called "received view" in natural science has been called into question by many philosophers of science and rejected by the majority.[38] The "received view" is the position that there is an objective, external world order, a fixed natural law governing behavior, and *objective* description and measurement of observed facts. Considering even the most technical aspects of the process of measurement in any natural science, the philosopher of science Kurt Hübner has argued that all of the basic statements of science (observational and computational) have a theoretical content. All basic concepts and statements have meaning and content only within a theory. Says Hübner:

> A basic statement expresses either an obtained or an expected measurement of result. Instruments are required for this measurement. However, in order to use such instruments, in order to place trust in them we must already have a theory concerning the form and manner of their functioning. This holds even for the simplest instruments—as for example for a ruler we obviously presuppose that by changing location it undergoes no change or calculable change (thus presupposing a certain metrics), and if we

---

38. Suppe, *Structure of Scientific Theories*, 115–16.

use a telescope this requires the acceptance of certain ideas such as how light rays behave in particular media, etc. (i.e. it presupposes a certain optics). But if the measurement procedure is to have the meaning (Sinn) given above, then both a theory of the instruments employed and, moreover, a theory concerning the quantities to be measured must precede the measurement process, since the concept of the quantities in question is not given through some indeterminate kind of everyday experience, but rather can only be defined and determined in terms of a theory. A brief example: If we wish to carry out a measurement of the length of light waves, then we must in advance have a wave theory of light; further, with the aid of this theory and a theory concerning the measurement instrument, we must know how this instrument makes possible such a measurement of wavelengths; and third, we must know how to read the sought-after measurement value from the instrument.[39]

Facts and basic principles are parts of theories, according to Hübner; they are given in a framework and are dependent on it. Moreover, according to Hübner, this holds for all empirical science. Thus Hübner concludes: "There are no absolute scientific facts or absolutely valid fundamental principles upon which scientific statements or theories can be based in a strict sense, or by means of which such statements and theories can be justified with necessity."[40] A similar theme is sounded throughout Frederick Suppe's *The Structure of Scientific Theories*, in which the major critics of the "received view" present their cases.

4. The Debate About Macro-Evolutionism in the Natural Sciences

As for the debates that are current within natural science itself, here too much more is disputed about evolutionism than most let on or their confident assertions would indicate. The core claims of the natural scientific view are about the whole cosmic process of evolution from the inert to life and on to human beings. Allow me an example here from the implicit cosmic chronology presented in the book entitled *The Fourth Day*.[41] In it the author starts with the "big bang" of an inanimate quantum of dust

---

39. Hübner, *Critique of Scientific Theories*, 26.
40. Hübner, *Critique of Scientific Theories*, 106.
41. Van Till, *Fourth Day*.

The Eclipse of Creation

and energy fifteen billion years ago,[42] and then goes on to a subsequent appearance of the Milky Way Galaxy ten billion years ago.[43] Finally the author goes on to the temporal evolution of life-forms that "follows from the properties and behavior of matter in a way that is similar to the processes that lead to the birth of planets, stars, and galaxies."[44] Not only does the author ignore religious and scientific reasons against this view, but he also expresses confidence, as Darwin once did over 150 years ago, "that a fully satisfactory description for the processes of biological evolution will eventually be worked out."[45] The author is counting on a description that will show that this evolution too "proceeds in a causally continuous manner ... [rather than] by arbitrary, discontinuous acts unrelated to the ordinary patterned behavior of matter."[46]

Apart from evidence against these views from a biblical perspective or based on Christian control beliefs, it is a matter of record that many scientists dispute the metaphysical and macro-evolutionistic claim that life evolved naturally and continuously from matter according to physical law over a vastly extended period of time. It is also a matter of record that the question of human descent is almost totally undecided. On both of these matters just cited, a large number of scientists who intentionally avoid dogmatic views and strive to be truly empirical argue that the evidence only allows us to conclude that there is a *discontinuous architecture of the inorganic, organic and human realms*. In the history of the natural sciences, claims that go beyond these results also go beyond commonsense human experience in the life world and must thus be judged to be hypothetical. Furthermore, if these claims are held as deductively or logically true so that they guide research, they must also be seen as dogmatic and speculative. To go beyond that entangles the researcher in poor science as well as religious control beliefs that are unwarranted.

One could think at this point of the famous medical scientist Louis Pasteur. Around the time of Darwin's publication of the *On the Origin of the Species by Means of Natural Selection or The Preservation of Favored Races in the Struggle for Life*, Pasteur was testing the ability of water to develop microbes out of direct contact with air. His experimental results were

---

42. Van Till, *Fourth Day*, 180.
43. Van Till, *Fourth Day*, 170.
44. Van Till, *Fourth Day*, 188.
45. Van Till, *Fourth Day*, 188.
46. Van Till, *Fourth Day*, 188.

totally negative, leading Pasteur to conclude that the idea of the spontaneous generation of life had been dealt a blow.[47] Wherever life develops, in Pasteur's case in the form of infusoria, he concluded that *for all we can know on the basis of the evidence*, it always develops from spores or original germs of life.

Though new circumstances in the natural sciences since Pasteur's time have offered other avenues to pursue in the search for the origin of life, this crucial link in the evolutionary process continues to be hotly contested. The assertion that there is a continuous evolution of all things from the properties of matter continues to be based on faith, and the theories about it continue to be derived with control beliefs that originate from a faith commitment. In most cases this theory of the spontaneous generation of life out of matter is a uniformity principle thought out to its logical conclusion and applied exhaustively to everything. It is not based on sight or empirical evidence.

Among the original theoreticians of evolutionism, such as Charles Darwin in England and Ernst Haeckel in Germany, the idea of the spontaneous generation of so-called "monera" was accepted. These "monera" are plasma bodies with organs that arose from inorganic materials through processes of chemical synthesis. They were regarded as the basic building blocks of life, the primeval slime from which life had evolved. Jon Lever in his history of the biological idea of the origin of life has demonstrated that this view was of short duration and very soon "it was affirmed that a grandiose mistake had been made. The *Bathybius Haeckelii* proved to be an artifact that results when sea water and alcohol are mixed, a gypsum-like sediment."[48]

In the twentieth century many evolutionistic thinkers in pursuit of an evolutionary theory followed the lead of the famous Russian scientist A. I. Oparin.[49] In his conception, organic "monomers" were formed as a result of reactions of solar radiation with compounds in the atmosphere and the waters. Through a complex of stages, eventually the first primitive cells appeared. Yet, here too, although popular texts witness to Oparin's testimony, a convicted evolutionist like Francis Crick, famous for winning the Nobel Prize for his research on DNA, contends that "the origin of life appears at

---

47. Wikipedia, "Louis Pasteur."
48. Lever, *Creation and Evolution*, 40.
49. Oparin, *Origin of Life on Earth*.

the moment to be almost a miracle."[50] Many evolutionists admit that the transition from the simple "monomers" and "polymers" of organic life to the cell is presently to be viewed as "improbable."[51]

With the discovery of viruses in the twentieth century many evolutionists believed that finally a cellular form had been discovered that could be regarded as "in between" living and nonliving things. Over time in this area of research too much dispute has developed. For example, viruses are in between organisms that do not "live" apart from a host; the host organism must be there first for viruses to exist. If viruses presuppose living organisms, their capacity as transitional forms between nonliving and living entities begs the question.

The most common contemporary view among evolutionists is the biochemical view. It shies away from the notion of spontaneous generation and proposes instead that the evolutionary route from inert material to the living entities is characterized by a very *gradual* succession of chemical compounds which, in interaction with the atmosphere, produce amino acids and proteins, the basic building blocks of life.

An evolutionary theory that begins with "life" soon runs into problems concerning the various complex forms of it. In this context Darwin's *Origin of the Species* has dominated the discussion. It assumes that the whole variety of living things represents a line of descent. Moreover, it uses the famous principle of natural selection to explain the process of speciation or the emergence of new and distinct species. Darwin's position is quite simple: nature selects those organisms best suited to survive the struggle for existence, thus resulting in the gradual improvement of each organic species and the emergence of new species.

This principle as stated has been demonstrated to be tautological: individuals adapted to survive have the best chance to survive. The claim itself did not survive long in science. Neo-Darwinians, not too much bothered by this problem, soon moved on to stress mutation and genetic inheritance as the agents of speciation. Current theories claim that when environmental barriers split gene pools leading to separation that prevents interbreeding, two or more species may survive. Even with these modifications, primary speciation in the form of two or more new species arising from an existing one has never been observed. Furthermore, the most common explanation

---

50. Crick, *Life Itself*, 88.
51. Mayr, *Growth of Biological Thought*, 584.

given for the lack of evidence is that primary speciation likely takes a very long time, up to one hundred thousand years.

While some scientists vigorously pursued this explanation and went off in search of the missing example that would demonstrate their view, others have become increasingly critical of it because the search has not turned up sufficient evidence to support the theory.[52] "The transformation of a basic genotype into another one as a result of a series of unidirectional mutations cannot be produced experimentally," the paleontologist Duyvene de Wit has argued. In the field of genetics, according to de Wit, the neo-Darwinian assumption that mutations contribute essentially to adaptive improvements in a sustained series of successive speciation is indefensible. Though new species may arise from polygenetic stock, these prove to "own a *pauperized* gene pool" that results in "genetic drift." In the end, the tragic fate of new groups attaining the taxonomic status of new species or genera is "genetic death." Thus, according to de Wit, far from representing evolution as progressive, as an onward and upward process of improvement and line of ascent, "the history of our organic world is, in fact, in spite of the relative constancy of the biomass, a succession of extinctions of species along with an expansion of only a few fortunate ones."[53]

Appealing to the prominent transformationalist paleontologist G. G. Simpson, de Wit argues that "all the basic organic types originated discontinuously," that is, appeared suddenly on earth in different localities and at different times. Simpson's interesting admissions, based on a nondogmatic reading of the evidence, merit full citation according to de Wit:

> Essentially continuous transitional sequences are virtually absent. This is true of all the 32 orders of mammals. The earliest and most primitive known members of every order already have the basic ordinal characters, and in no case is an approximately continuous sequence from one order to another known. The regular absence of transitional forms is not confined to mammals alone, but is an almost universal phenomenon, as has long been noted by paleontologists. It is true of almost all orders of all classes of animals, both vertebrate and invertebrate. A fortiori, it is also true of the classes themselves, and of the major animal phyla, and it is apparently also true of analogous categories of plants. The gaps between the higher categories do not merely represent artifacts, but are of a systematic nature. None of the larger breaks has actually been

---

52. Lewontin, *Genetic Basis of Evolutionary Change*, 159.
53. de Wit, "Paleontological Record," 6–8.

filled by real, continuous sequences of fossils, although many of these gaps can be exactly located. The reality of their existence cannot be doubted.

In this evolutionary portrayal, de Wit concludes, the transformation of the species has not risen above the level of hypothesis according to Simpson's own admission. In short it has become a metaphysical principle of "logical necessity" superimposed on the empirical evidence of the organic world.[54]

As for the paleontological record and the origin of humans, de Wit's own area of expertise, the evidence for the general evolutionistic theory has proved no more promising than the results of genetic biology. According to de Wit, whose own locale of research has been the site of some of the most significant skeletal finds, any idea, first of all, that human prehistory can be reconstructed from an examination of fossil remains is fatuous. Furthermore, according to de Wit, sufficient fossil documentation is lacking with respect to the assumed animal ancestors of humankind.

Finally, according to de Wit, many empirical discoveries by paleontologists have created dialectical knots and jams for the evolutionistic theory of the descent of humans from animals. For example, paleontologists have discovered relatively highly developed, human-looking races that existed more than a half million years *before* the Australopithecines, or the Southern ape-men, but since evolution is viewed as progressive and irreversible this has meant that these ape-men could not serve as a model of the earliest type of human, as they had for the standard evolutionistic theories of the descent of humans from animals.

Since the search for missing links between the animal kingdom and human beings continues to sustain serious blows of this kind, de Wit, guided by the creation-fall-redemption theme of Scripture, has himself offered an alternative, nontransformationist construal of the empirical data. His view correlates well with the results of genetics, namely that the future of any new species is extinction due to genetic pauperization. In this connection, de Wit's own words merit citation:

> The revealed fall of the whole of mankind into sin necessarily implies a general spiritual uprooting of a large part of the very earliest human family, as a consequence of its turning away from God, the Creator and absolute Origin of all. Delivered to the hostilities of nature, a selective natural premium was set on genetic adaptation of the human phenotype towards a large diversity of ecological

54. de Wit, "Paleontological Record," 8–9.

> conditions. Raciation was the consequence of the process, and in some races, as, for instance, the Southern Ape-men, a regressive process of phenotypical brutification and devolution has apparently proceeded to such an extent that convergent similarities with the morphology of the higher animal primates has developed. This convergent morphological regression reflects the earlier mentioned enormous genetic polymorphy of the human species and has nothing to do with the genetic endowments of the animal primates as postulated by the transformist doctrine. For this reason the microcephalic and cannibalic Australanthropines can and may not be advanced as a "model" of the earliest Phenotype of man . . . . [Thus] I consider certain displays at the exhibition "Man in Africa" at Johannesburg as scientifically misleading for the same reason. This exhibition was daily visited by hundreds of school-going children in whose minds the mythical doctrine of the animal descent of man became imprinted.[55]

Finally important evidence comes from taxonomy, the specialty in biology which systematically investigates the linking of large varieties and classes of species to common ancestors. The research there yields the same negative results with respect to the main claims about continuity, transformationism, and speciation in evolutionistic theory.

An article by Tom Bethell, a science journalist, reviews some of the challenges to the theory of evolutionism issuing from a school of British taxonomists known as "cladists." These scientists accuse evolutionists of slipshod methods and sloppy science. As Bethell reports the controversy, the battle cry of the cladists is: "The concept of ancestry is not accessible to the tools we have." Accordingly common ancestors can only be *hypothesized*, not identified in the fossil record. What can be discerned in nature according to the cladists are patterns, but no processes or parent-offspring links. The cladists conclude, according to Bethell that "the science of evolution is in large part a matter of faith, faith different, but not all *that* different, from that of the creationists."[56]

So it seems that the most important features of the modern theory of macro-evolutionism cannot be experimentally corroborated by evidence within the lifetime of any one scientist, as was the case with Darwin. Defenders of the theory of evolutionism are placed in an awkward position because their explanation for the origin of the species must be accepted

---

55. de Wit, "Paleontological Record," 16.
56. Bethell, "Agnostic Evolutionists," 52.

largely on faith. In fact, it must be accepted on faith for what is, for all practical purposes, an indefinite period of time. If corroboration has not been forthcoming for more than 150 years, the theory is sufficiently vague to require at least an additional 150,000 years because the evolution claimed will happen so slowly that no scientists can observe it in their own lifetimes.

Thus the modern theory of evolutionism, to the extent that it attempts to explain the origin of the species, leaves the realm of experimental natural science and begins to sound like eschatology. Religious claims for the parousia may be empirically verifiable in less time than it takes to test the modern mythology of macro-evolutionism. Considering the extreme uncertainty about the essential mechanism of primary speciation, any claim about macro-evolution from matter to human life seems extravagant, to say the least. It seems to me that science might be better served by acknowledging, at a minimum, the *hypothetical* status of the modern theory of metaphysical evolutionism.

Much more serious than the special theory of speciation is the general theory of evolutionism that extrapolates from speciation to the idea that humankind developed through a series of successive speciations. The theory claims that from a primal substratum of basic matter evolving, humans came after animals, animals came after plants and simple organic life, and plants came after inanimate matter. Furthermore, adding logic defying fuel to the fire by assuming that "coming after" also literally means "coming out of," the progression of ideas is thrown into the realm of the unwarranted and unbelievable. Here we are not talking about whales turning into horses, but humans being a part of an alleged general process of evolution. Finally then for complementarists and concordists to go even further to claim that this coming discovery is compatible with the Christian and biblical idea of creation because it will inform us regarding *how* God created humans, it appears that the theory puts an indigestible frosting on an inedible cake. How could there be a more disconcerting and widespread eclipse of the biblical story of creation than the one we have seen taking place in the twentieth and twenty-first centuries?

Not only do I believe the principle of a continuous stream of matter to be obviously *meta*-physical; it is mythological as well. By this I do not mean only to suggest that it is a recent faith or a belief. It is in fact a belief that has come to us historically from ancient, primitive stories around the time of the pre-Socratic Greeks and first millennium Romans. It is a mythic imagination that expressly contradicts the narrative of Gen 1 and 2 with its stress on the themes of separation, division, and discontinuity. In Scripture differentiation is cosmologically basic and irreducible.

The idea of a universal cosmic continuity honors the sorts of metamorphoses that fascinated many ancients, other than the anti-mythological philosophers of the time. Differentiation within the cosmic order was for these ancient mythologizers inherently unstable, requiring storied enforcement because it was not, according to them, sustained in the nature of things. For example, in Ovid's poem *Metamorphosis*,[57] Caesar is transubstantiated into a star, boulders are metamorphosed into children, and ants are transformed into the people called Myrmidons. But mainly Ovid's human beings devolve into animals. The phenomenally given primal order of things is unstable, fluid, apparent, and thus essentially inauthentic. Moreover, this ancient mythic sensibility is mediated to modern times through medieval folklore and the legends of the fairy tales, which are replete with transfigurations that easily cross the boundary between human beings and animals. Modern evolutionistic theory bears this same motif. No modern view does more powerfully exactly what the folklore of the past has done than macro-evolutionism with its continuous evolution of matter.

The primitive idea of unity and fluid boundaries among things is a subtle pagan conviction rarely brought to words in modern natural science. Yet the primitive religious factor remains but without our being conscious of it, because we have superimposed on it a web of allegedly "objective" scientific theories. Natural scientists claim that they are not poets or mythologizers, but evolutionistic natural science has a greater chance of being grounded in myth and poetry than its practitioners may imagine. As Steven Toulmin has said, the difference between times past and modernity is not that the primitives had their myths and we do not, but that we, unlike our ancestors, derive our myths from modern science.[58]

One more question remains about "matter evolving." The famous modern physicist Stephen Hawking has said that the cosmic system has from the "beginning" been governed by "physical law." The basic speck of dust and energy has all along evolved according to the elementary law of physics, which was continuous and universal. According to Hawking any doubt about this is groundless.[59] But obvious questions do occur. Does and

---

57. Thought to originate in approximately AD 8.
58. Toulmin, *Return to Cosmology*, 21–81.
59. Hawking, *Brief Answers to Big Questions*.

did this "law" exist outside of the process? Or is this question a dated conception of invariant law governing changing functional behavior?

In modern science the reigning concept of invariant physical law has given way to the model of evolutionism too. In fact evolutionistic scientists have themselves rendered the classical Newtonian and Scholastic views of law obsolete in their attempts to show its incompatibility with the process of evolution. Modern science has moved on to a more current and self-consistent phase, and accordingly many scientists now reject the epistemological claim that knowledge in physics merits the status of objectivity.

A good example of such current evolutionistic theory is present in Ilya Prigogine's book *Order Out of Chaos*. I cannot do justice to the book's entire theory, but at least some of Prigogine's musings merit consideration here. According to Prigogine, classical modern science thinks in terms of behavior and time-independent laws. In addition, according to the classical view, the simplest nearby phenomena reveal the key to nature as a whole. The idea of the rational order of the universe lies at the heart of classical seventeenth-century science, an idea grounded in the medieval theological idea of God as providing a basis for the world's intelligibility. According to Prigogine, scholastic theology and modern science converge on this notion.

More recently modern science has outlived its moment of cultural consonance with theology. According to Prigogine, "temporality has invaded classical science." Moreover, thermodynamics has introduced the concept of dissipative change or entropy, so that in physics there is room to acknowledge that many physical processes are "irreversible." They are in effect dissipative, neither repeatable nor retraceable according to fixed physical law. According to Prigogine, physics is thus developing a more biological view of law and behavior as well as the interrelation of the two. Randomness and irreversibility are the rule. Prigogine speaks strongly of the "delusion of the universal." Physical structures seem to adapt to circumstances, and in nonequilibrium states matter appears able "to take into account."[60] According to Prigogine, time has been introduced into physics, suggesting dissipation as well as progress.

In Prigogine's view law itself must be subjected to the concept of process. Why should anything be exempted from the model of evolution except for arbitrary reasons? Rather than speak of law obtaining absolutely and invariantly for matter, Prigogine advocates the notion of emergent structures. Moreover, since process can mean dissipation, fluctuations and

---

60. Prigogine and Stengers, *Order Out of Chaos*, 5–14.

deviations that threaten the stability of physical systems are the basis of the new order.[61]

Physics itself verifies empirically that the universe is not an absolutely coherent system governed by continuous and universal law. New structures emerge out of the sometimes radical fluctuations of the system. Accordingly, Prigogine accepts the reality of fundamental contingency and uncertainty, and he promotes the idea of an evolving law.[62]

I cannot consider here what the notion of process and evolution has meant for epistemology. This too should be, and in fact has been, considered in contemporary physics. Suffice it to say here that many physicists, among whom David Bohm is the most well known, disown altogether the idea of objective science because of a consistent application of evolutionism to their view of knowledge itself.[63]

Now I claim personally neither to accept nor reject these views, but it is clear that they are viewed by their advocates as implications of evolutionism. The question for theistic or concordist evolutionists is whether they are aware of the tension that exists between the evolutionist content of their position and the Scholastic and positivist view of knowledge they also at the same time continue to promote. Do they promote it despite developments within their own disciplines? Can one consistently have it both ways, as both-and, Christian, synthetic thinkers would suggest? Or does both-and thinking in the long run force its adherents to think generally more consequentially, as Prigogine and Bohm apparently have? Darwin himself began to do this over the course of his career, moving from a Christian Unitarianism, to theism, and finally to explicit agnosticism, denying that there had ever been any kind of revelation from God.

Finally, none should disregard the enormous personal bigotry that Darwin took for granted in his work to establish the so-called scientific principle of the survival of the fittest. In fact the full title of Darwin's first book is *On the Origin of Species by Means of Natural Selection, or the Preservation of Favored Races in the Struggle for Life*.[64] A similar critique of Darwin's "pure reason" was articulated by the philosophical ethicist Cecil de Boer in his defense of ethics as an irreducible human center of identity and

---

61. Prigogine and Stengers, *Order Out of Chaos*, 178.
62. Prigogine and Stengers, *Order Out of Chaos*, 209.
63. Bohm, *Wholeness and the Implicit Order* 48–62.
64. Referenced by Marilynne Robinson's hard-nosed rejection of metaphysical evolutionism in her book *Death of Adam*, 43.

activity. In his *The If's and Ought's of Ethics: A Preface to Moral Philosophy*, he writes:

> Nevertheless it would seem rather clear that the consciousness of values, their choice and preservation, signifies a set of facts belonging to an entirely new dimension of existence. However, no amount of argument will convince anybody already convinced in the other direction; and if the evolutionist is ready to assert that the Sermon on the Mount and Brahm's Symphony in C Minor receive their ultimate significance from the facts of natural selection and the survival of the fittest, there is nothing more to be said. No argument can avail against a faith that removes mountains.[65]

---

65. De Boer, *If's and Ought's of Ethics*, 155.

Conclusion

Creation as the Foundation of Christian Thought

OVER TIME IN THE COURSE of western Judaism and Christianity, we have witnessed the rise and fall of their foundation in creation thought. As a Christian, I am profoundly grateful to the religion of Judaism and its canonic revelation for bequeathing creation thought to Western civilization. The scrolls ("bible") of Yeshua of Nazareth founded and grounded his faith and reason. He did not desire a jot or tittle of it to be undone by either his preaching or by his God-sent work. Nevertheless, in the subsequent centuries, we have witnessed its diminishment through accommodation to "natural reason" and "natural theology."

In addition we have witnessed its partial suffocation in the Enlightenment's norming of its truth by what was taken to be reasonable and scientific. The study of "Reality" and what it is was taken over by the scientific revolution; and then taken a step further in the philosophy of Kant. Religion was reduced to the three principles of the pure practical reason (god, freedom, and immortality), not truths, but a system of *values* for the maintenance of a stable society. In modern anti-Semitism, Christians like John Calvin who sought to give the Father, almighty maker of heaven and earth, his proper and first place role were accused of being "Judaizers."

Ages old Gnosticism reared its heretical head by viewing this worldly abode as having only temporary relevance; we are born in a cave, and we are gradually making our way out as we acquire the proper gnosis. Plato and his contemporaries talked that way: our temporal abode is a vale of tears from which we will be freed when we perish and return to the ideal realm from which we came. In addition there are many recent ways to eclipse creation, one of which is a widespread, lowbrow reduction of Christian faith to a "personal relationship with Jesus," or to the notion that is often hailed

Conclusion

with the slogan "Jesus Saves." We cannot expect the survival of Christianity in our rapidly secularizing culture, if we allow the secular world to dictate to us what should become of culture.

A higher brow version of Christological Unitarianism emerged in the twentieth century in the European world. Important theologians have written about the *Eclipse of Creation* and *The Death of the Old Testament*. We would be wise to heed their warnings regarding the progression toward the death of God in modern Western culture. In the Netherlands, in what was at one time one of the most explicitly religious countries of Europe, one can now see scores of Christian churches turned into shopping centers and restaurants, while the churches that remain open attract only about 3 percent of the Dutch population for weekly worship. Similar trends may be seen in other countries of Western Europe as well.

Last but not least the rise of modern *meta*-physical evolutionism, taught in public schools everywhere, has dealt a final blow to Christian creation thought. Within the Christian tradition this has given rise to a putative "have it both ways" view that erodes Christian control beliefs and leads to the neglect of foundational faith content. Significant among these changes are altered beliefs about an original state of rectitude in which the persons Adam and Eve dwelt and from which they fell into sin. Dealing with such content is simply too awkward, and as a result it is rarely mentioned in the churches.

Within the Christian community one must wonder about the rise of a "Christ of culture" Christianity that continuously forces the Christian community to accommodate its message to what's out there if it is going to remain acceptable. At the hands of Christian theologians and natural scientists working in Christian institutions, we have witnessed the consignment of biblical data, presented in narrative and storied form, to incidentals. Why these and such like restrictions? Why too the preference, often carried out by means of text manipulation, for a view of creation as an ongoing activity rather than the primary creation out of nothing of an original, differentiated heavens and earth which God finished after the sixth "day"?

Why the blurring of the boundaries between creation as a once-for-all act of establishment in the beginning, called *in principio* in the Vulgate, which God "finished because he was done" and ongoing "creation," the constant, subsequent copresence of God to the world in preservation and governance? Why the modern revision of the idea of "origins" rendering the concept of God as the "eternal ground" of the covenant, and why the corresponding consignment of the question of origins in the temporal and formal sense to natural science? Why the persistent subordination of the faith content and importance of creation out of nothing to continuing creation? And why the subtle pushing of the message of a first perfect creation into, above all, a message of "saving responsiveness," which is then rendered in theologies of hope as a vision of the eschatological coming of the first perfect kingdom? Why finally a putative return to creation understood now as an ecological concern for creation care when the real, hard-hitting cultural mandate from the Creator to humans in the beginning was "to be fruitful, to multiply, to replenish the earth, to subdue it, and to exercise dominion over it"?

The study of reality in all of its aspects, using as a framework the Christian control beliefs about creation that come first in the order of right biblical teaching, is the help needed for the Christian community to bring faith to life in every area. I have called the tool to comprehend and accomplish this Christian philosophy, a comprehensive Christian educational enterprise. The perspective with which Christian believers are raised in the community of faith needs to be applied to the study of creation realities if this vision is to be achieved. Christian education at all levels has become the new mission field. This approach will be necessary if there is to be hope for breaking away from the catastrophic secularization of life that has taken place in the modern world and the public square. I leave the reader with these reflections. Give it some thought. "Always be ready to give a defense to everyone who asks you a reason for the hope that is in you" (1 Pet 3:15).

Bibliography

Allen, Michael. "Theological Theology." *First Things*, Nov. 1, 2020, 19–23.
Anderson, Bernhard. *Creation Versus Chaos: The Reinterpretation of Mythical Symbolism in the Bible.* New York: Association Press, 1967.
Augustine of Hippo. *City of God.* Translated by John Hammond Taylor. Garden City, NY: Image Books, 1958.
———. *The Literal Meaning of Genesis.* Translated by John Hammond Taylor. Vol. 1. New York: Newman Press, 1982.
Barth, Karl. *Church Dogmatics.* Vols. 3/1–4. Edinburgh: T & T Clark, 1956–60.
———. *Dogmatics in Outline.* New York: Harper & Row, 1959.
———. *The German Church Conflict.* Cambridge, UK: Lutterworth, 2008.
———. *Revolutionary Theology in the Making: Barth-Thurnesysen Correspondence 1914–1925.* Translated by James Smart. Louisville: John Knox, 1964.
Bavinck, Herman. *Gereformeerde Dogmatiek.* Vol. 2. Kampen: Kok, 1928.
———. *Reformed Dogmatics. Vol. 2, God and Creation.* Grand Rapids: Baker Academic, 2004.
Bethell, Tom. "Agnostic Evolutionist." *Harper's Magazine* (Feb. 1983) 49–61.
———. *Darwin's House of Cards.* Seattle: Discovery Institute, 2016.
Boer, H. "Arbitrary Nonsense." *Reformed Journal* 38.4 (Apr. 1988) 3–4.
Bohm, David. *Wholeness and the Implicit Order.* Boston: Routledge and Kegan Paul, 1980.
Bonhoeffer, Dietrich. *Creation and Fall.* New York: Macmillan, 1966.
Bouwsma, William. *John Calvin: A Sixteenth Century Portrait.* New York: Oxford University Press, 1988.
Bultmann, Rudolf. "New Testament and Mythology." In *Kerygma and Myth: A Theological Debate*, edited by Hans Werner Bartsch. New York: Harper Torchbook, 1961.
Calvin, John. *Commentaries on the Book of Genesis* Vol. 1. Grand Rapids: Eerdmans, 1948.
———. "Commentary on 1 Peter 2." Calvin's Commentaries on the Bible, Study Light. https://www.studylight.org/commentaries/eng/cal/1-peter-2.html.
———. *Institutes of the Christian Religion.* Translated by Ford Lewis Battles. 1559 ed. Philadelphia: Westminster, 1960.
———. *New Testament Commentaries on Hebrews, and I and II Peter.* Grand Rapids: Eerdmans, 1994.
Chandra, Avinash. *The Scientist and the Saint: The Limits of Science and the Testimony of the Sages.* Cambridge, UK: Chetwynd House, 2018.
Clouser, Roy. *The Myth of Religious Neutrality: Essays on the Hidden Role of Religious Beliefs in Theories.* South Bend, IN: University of Notre Dame Press, 1991.

Bibliography

Cochrane, Arthur C. *The Church's Confession Under Hitler*. Philadelphia: Westminster, 1962.

Conway, John S. *The Nazi Persecution of the Churches, 1933–1945*. Vancouver: Regent College Publishing, 1997.

Crick, Francis. *Life Itself*. London: MacDonald, 1982.

Currid, John. *Genesis: Volume 1*. Grand Rapids: Evangelical Press, 2015.

Cusanus, Nicholas. *Of Learned Ignorance*. Eugene, OR: Wipf & Stock, 2007.

De Boer, Cecil. *The If's and Ought's of Ethics: A Preface to Modern Philosophy*. Grand Rapids: Eerdmans, 1936.

Deloria, Vine, Jr. *Evolution, Creationism, and Other Modern Myths*. Golden, CO: Fulcrum, 2002.

———. *God Is Red: A Native View of Religion*. Wheat Ridge, CO: Fulcrum, 2003.

DeWit, Duyvene. *A New Critique of the Transformist Principle in Evolutionary Biology*. Kampen: Kok, 1965.

———. "The Paleontological Record and the Origin of Man." Paper presented at Proceedings of the Scientific Society of the University of the Orange Free State, 1963.

Diemer, Johan. *Nature and Miracle*. Toronto: Wedge Publishing Foundation, 1977.

Dooyeweerd, Herman. *A New Critique of Theoretical Thought*. Vols. 1 and 2. Philadelphia: Presbyterian and Reformed, 1955.

———. "Schepping en Evolutie." *Philosophia Reformata* 24 (1959) 113–59.

Douglas, Mary. *Purity and Danger*. London: Routledge and Kegan Paul, 1966.

Ehrhardt, Arnold T. "Christianity and Law." *Scottish Journal of Theology* 15.3 (1962) 305–10.

Florovsky, Georges. *Creation and Redemption, Volume Three*. Belmont, MA: Nordland, 1976.

Frei, Hans. *Eclipse of the Biblical Narrative: A Study in 18th and 19th Century Hermeneutics*. New Haven, CT: Yale University Press, 1974.

Gibson, John. *Genesis*. Vol. 1. Louisville: Westminster John Knox, 1981.

Gilbert, Elizabeth. *City of Girls*. New York: Random House, 2019.

Gilkey, Langdon. *Maker of Heaven and Earth*. Garden City, NY: Doubleday, 1959.

Gispen, W. H. *Schepping en Paradijs*. Kampen: Kok, 1966.

Greenblatt, Stephen. *The Rise and Fall of Adam and Eve*. New York: Norton, 2017.

———. *The Swerve: How the World Became Modern*. New York: Norton, 2011.

Haarsma, Deborah, and Loren D. Haarsma. *Origins: Christian Perspectives on Creation, Evolution, and Intelligent Design*. Grand Rapids: Faith Alive Christian Resources, 2011.

Hart, David Bentley. "Reason's Faith." *First Things*, Mar. 2015.

Hawking, Stephen. *Brief Answers to Big Questions*. New York: Bantam, 2018.

Hendry, George. *Theology of Nature*. Philadelphia: Westminster, 1980.

Hudson, Liam. *The Cult of the Fact*. New York: Harper, 1972.

Hübner, Kurt. *Critique of Scientific Theories*. Chicago: University of Chicago Press, 1983.

Hunter, Cornelius. *Darwin's God: Evolution and the Problem of Evil*. Grand Rapids: Brazos, 2001.

Inman, Ross. *Christian Philosophy as a Way of Life*. Grand Rapids: Baker Academic, 2023.

Johnson, Paul. *A History of the Jews*. New York: Harper and Row, 1987.

Jonas, Hans. *The Gnostic Religion*. Boston: Beacon, 1963.

Kant, Immanuel. *Critique of Practical Reason*. London: Merchant Books, 2009.

———. *Critique of Pure Reason*. New York: Macmillan, 1925.

Bibliography

Kass, Leon. "Evolution and the Bible: Genesis 1 Revisited." *Commentary*, Nov. 1, 1988, 29–39.
Kelly, J. N. D. *Early Christian Creeds*. London: Longmans, Green, and Company, 1950.
Kuhn, Thomas. *The Structure of Scientific Revolutions*. Chicago: University of Chicago Press, 2012.
Kuyper, Abraham. *Destruction of Boundaries*. Translated by J. Hendrik de Vries. Hungerford, UK: Legare Street, 2022.
———. "Evolution." *Calvin Theological Journal* (Apr. 1996) 11–50.
———. *Ijzer en Leem*. Amsterdam: J. H. Kruyt, 1885.
———. *De Verflauwing der Grenzen*. Amsterdam: J. A. Wormser, 1892.
Lever, Jon. *Creation and Evolution*. Grand Rapids: International Publications, 1958.
Levering, Matthew. *Engaging the Doctrine of Creation: Cosmos, Creatures, and the Wise and Good Creator*. Grand Rapids: Baker Academic, 2017.
Lewis, C. S. *The Screwtape Letters*. New York: Touchstone, 1996.
Lewontin, Richard. *The Genetic Bias of Evolutionary Change*. New York: Columbia University Press, 1974.
Luther, Martin. *Lectures on Genesis*. Vol. 1 of *Luther's Works*. St. Louis: Concordia and Fortress, 1958.
Maimonides, Moses. *The Guide to the Perplexed: A New Translation*. Stanford, CA: Stanford University Press, 2024.
Mayr, Ernst. *The Growth of Biological Thought*. Cambridge, MA: Harvard University Press, 1982.
Midgley, Mary. *Evolution as a Religion*. London: Routledge Classics, 2002.
Moberly, R. W. L. *The Bible in a Disenchanted Age: The Enduring Possibility of Christian Faith*. Grand Rapids: Baker, 2018.
———. *Old Testament Theology. Reading the Hebrew Bible as Christian Scripture*. Grand Rapids: Baker, 2013.
Moltmann, Jürgen. *The Future of Creation*. Philadelphia: Fortress, 1974.
Morris, Henry. *The World Is Made of Glass*. Sydney: Allen and Unwin, 2017.
Niebuhr, H. Richard. *Christ and Culture*. New York: Harper, 1975.
Oparin, Alexander. *Origin of Life on Earth*. New York: Macmillan, 1938.
Patterson, Stephen, et al. *The Search for Jesus: Modern Scholarship Looks at the Gospels*. Edited by Shanks Hershel. Washington, DC: Biblical Archaeology Society, 1994.
Paulson, Steven. *Atoms and Eden*. Oxford: Oxford University Press, 2010.
Plantinga, Alvin. *Where the Conflict Really Lies: Science, Religion, and Naturalism*. Oxford: Oxford University Press, 2011.
Plantinga, Richard, et al. *An Introduction of Christian Theology*. Cambridge, UK: Cambridge University Press, 2023.
Prigogine, Ilya, and Isabelle Stengers. *Order Out of Chaos: Man's New Dialogue with Nature*. New York: Bantam, 1984.
Rappoport, Angelo. *Myths and Legends of Ancient Israel*. New York: Bonanza Books, 1987.
Richards, Robert, and Michael Ruse. *Debating Darwin*. Chicago: University of Chicago Press, 2016.
Richardson, Herbert. *Toward an American Theology*. London: Harper, 1967.
Robinson, Marilyn. *The Death of Adam: Essays on Modern Thought*. New York: Picador, 2005.
Rosenblatt, Naomi. *After the Apple*. New York: Miramax: 2005.

Bibliography

Runner, H. Evan. *Walking in the Way of the Word: The Collected Writings of W. Evan Runner.* Vol. 1. Grand Rapids: Paideia Press, 2016.

Schleiermacher, Friedrich. *The Christian Faith.* Edinburgh: T & T Clark, 1968.

Smith, Christian. *Soul Searching: The Religious and Spiritual Lives of American Teenagers.* Oxford: Oxford University Press, 2009.

Spykman, Gordon. "Beginnings—A Few Thoughts in Passing." *Dialogue* 18.3 (Dec. 1985) 6–11.

Strauss, Leo. "Interpretation of Genesis." *L'Homme* 21.1 (Jan.–Mar. 1981) 5–20.

Strawn, Brent. *The Old Testament Is Dying.* Grand Rapids: Baker Academic, 2017.

Suppe, Frederick, ed. *The Structure of Scientific Theories.* Urbana: University of Illinois Press, 1979.

Sweetman, Robert. *Tracing the Lines: Spiritual Exercise and the Gestures of Christian Scholarship.* Eugene, OR: Wipf & Stock, 2016.

Taylor, Ian. *In The Minds of Men: Darwin and the New World Order.* Toronto: TFE Publishing, 1987.

Tilgner, Wolfgang. *Volksnomostheologies und Schöpfungsglaube: Ein Betrag zur Geschichte des Kirkenkampfes.* Göttingen: Vanderhoeck and Ruprecht, 1965.

Toulmin, Stephen. *The Return to Cosmology.* Berkeley: University of California Press, 1985.

Tyson, Paul. *A Christian Theology of Science: Reimagining a Theological Vision of Natural Knowledge.* Grand Rapids: Baker Academic, 2022.

Vander Goot, Henry. *Interpreting the Bible in Theology and the Church.* Lewiston, NY: Edwin Mellen, 1984.

———, ed. *Life Is Religion: Essay in Honor of H. Evan Runner.* Vol 1. St. Catherines, Ont.: Paideia Press, 1981.

Van Leeuwen, Raymond. "Liminality and Worldview in Proverbs 1–9." *Semeia* 50 (1990) 10–11.

Van Till, Howard. *The Fourth Day: What the Bible and the Heavens Are Telling Us About the Creation.* Grand Rapids: Eerdmans, 1986.

Voegelin, Eric. *Science, Politics, and Gnosticism.* Washington, DC: Regnery Gateway, 1997.

Von Rad, Gerhard. "The Theological Problem of the OT Doctrine of Creation." In *The Problem of the Hexateuch and Other Essays.* London: McGraw Hill, 1966.

Westermann, Claus. *Creation.* Philadelphia: Fortress, 1974.

———. *Genesis 1–11: A Commentary.* Minneapolis: Augsburg, 1987.

White, Lynn. "The Historical Roots of Our Ecological Crisis." *Science* 155.3767 (1967) 1203–7.

Wikipedia. "European Wars of Religion." https://en.wikipedia.org/wiki/European_wars_of_religion.

———. "Julius Wellhausen." https://en.wikipedia.org/wiki/Julius_Wellhausen.

———. "Louis Pasteur." https://en.wikipedia.org/wiki/Louis_Pasteur.

Wingren, Gustaf. "Den Springande Punkten." *Svensk Teologisk Kvartalskrift* 3 (1974) 101–7.

———. *Flight from Creation.* Minneapolis: Augsburg, 1971.

Wolterstorff, Nicholas. *Reason Within the Bounds of Religion.* Grand Rapids: Eerdmans, 1976.

Young, Norman. *Creation, Creator, and Faith.* London: Collins, 1976.

Zaslow, David. *Jesus: First Century Rabbi.* Brewster, MA: Paraclete, 2015.

Index

After the Apple (Rosenblatt), 9c
agape theology, 96
Allen, Michael, 21
Althaus, Paul, 100–101, 103
Anderson, Bernhard, 93
Aristotle, 7–8
Augustine, 54, 65, 73, 109–10

Barmen Confession, 98
Barth, Karl
   alternative revelation in disguise, 114
   Christomonistic Unitarianism and, 4
   evil, origination of, 91–92
   existentialist philosophy of encounter, 21
   German Church and, 96–103
   I-Thou encounter, 29, 84
   "nothingness" out of which God created, 59–60
Bathybius Haeckelii artifact, 122
Bavinck, Herman, 106, 108–9
Bekennende Kirche (Confessing Church), 98, 102
Belgic Confession, 4
Bethell, Tom, 126
Bible. *See* Scripture
Biblical Archaeology Society, 18
biblical directives, 78, 79
bibliocentrism, 23–24
Big Bang Theory, 79
biochemical view, 123
biological evolution, 121. *See also* Darwin, Charles
blessings, 71

The Blurring of the Boundaries (Kuyper), 67
Bonhoeffer, Dietrich, 67
book of nature, 26
Borg, Marcus, 18
Brief Answers to the Big Questions (Hawking), 79
Brunner, Emil, 98–99
Bultmann, Rudolf, 19

"Caesaro-Papist" controversies, 9
Calvin, John
   anti-Semitism and, 132
   on boundaries, limits, separations, and antitheses, 108
   commonsense experience, 69
   on creation, 65–66
   on fallen human beings, 114
   on higher power, 36–38
   human grasp of general revelation, 116
   image of a house analogy, 74–75
   Institutes of the Christian Religion, 5, 20–21, 33, 104–5
   on Moses' creation story, 61–62
   on mystery, 34
   oneness in Christ, 78
   Scripture in seeking God, 54
   spectacles, used for scripture, 5
   theater to describe creation, 74
   on Trinity, 81
   two-foldness of revelation, 24–25
   vain speculation, 52
categorical complementarism, 14

Index

Catholicism. *See* Roman Catholic Church
Chandra, Avinash, 6n13
Christian community, 133
Christian epistemology, 2
Christian ontology, 2
Christian philosophy
   bibliocentrism, 23–24
   creation as story, 25–28
   overview, 23
   real and legitimate, 29–30
   revelation, two-foldness of, 24–25, 31
   theology, necessity of, 30–32
   theology in need of, 28–29
Christian philosophy, as real and legitimate, 29–30
A Christian Theology of Science (Tyson), 31n3, 39
Christian Unitarianism, 130
Christological Unitarianism, 4, 60, 91, 133
Church, religion and, 9–10
Church Dogmatics (Barth), 92
City of Girls (Gilbert), 56, 90–91
cladists, 126
common grace, 6n13
concordism, 104, 114
Confessing Church (*Bekennende Kirche*), 98, 102
Confessions (Augustine), 65
Conway, John, 102
creatio continua, 58, 64–65, 80, 95, 107
creatio ex nihilo (creation out of nothing), 58–60, 92
creation
   biochemical view, 123
   evolutionism versus, 111–18
   as story, 25–28
   time and, 105–11
   as two-fold content of revelation, 31
Creation (Westermann), 93–94
Creation and Law (Wingren), 103
Creation Research Society, 27
Creation Science, 26
creational structures, 78
Crick, Francis, 122
"*cuius regio, euis religio*," 10

Darwin, Charles, 84, 115, 121–22, 123, 126, 130
day, defining of, 73–74
de Boer, Cecil, 130
De Jong, Ymen Peter, 16
De Koster, Lester, 27
De Verflauwing der Grenzen (Kuyper), 67, 109
de Wit, Duyvene, 124–26
death, mystery of, 34
Defense of the Faith (Van Til), 17
Deloria, Vine, Jr., 87, 106
Descartes, René, 69
Diemer J. H., 113
Ding an sich, 12, 13, 50
directional principle of unity in Christ, 78
division/separation differentiation, 65–72
"the doctrine of learned ignorance," 33
Dooyeweerd, Herman, 76, 87, 107, 113, 113n31
Douglas, Mary, 108
dualism, 7–8

ecclesiastical institution, Church as, 9
"Eclipse of Creation" (Wingren), 91
ecumenical creeds, of the Christian church, 61
Ehrhardt, Arnold T., 103
Eighty Years War, 10
Elder Testament
   death of, 133
   as Judaistic and judgmental, 59
   term usage, 2, 2n4
   two-foldness of, 24
Elert, Werner, 99, 100, 103
Epicurius, 115–16
"equality" mathematical term, 11
evil
   Barth on, 91–92
   good and, 55–57, 89
   Kant on, 13
   mystery of, 33, 38
evolution, as myth, 106
Evolution, Creationism, and Other Modern Myths (Deloria, Jr.), 87

Index

Evolution as a Religion (Midgley), 87, 106
evolutionism
   creation and time, 105–11
   creation versus, 111–18
   macro-evolutionist debate, 120–31
   natural sciences and, 118–20
   overview, 104–5
evolutionistic science, myth of, 79–80

"faith seeking understanding," 19
final solution of the Jewish problem, 97
first creation, waste and void, 60
first enlightenment, 11–12
first paradise, 91–95
First Things (journal), 15, 21
Flight from Creation (Wingren), 2
"forms of sensibility," 12
foundation in Christian thought, 132
The Fourth Day (Van Till), 120–21
The Future of Creation (Moltmann), 95

Galileo, 40
general revelation, 26
Genesis
   Moses, author of, 45–52
   story of, 34–35, 38
   use of week as sevenfold, 74–75
Genesis 1 and 2 lesson from
   all is very good, 55–57
   creator-creation distinction, 54–55
   speculation, against, 53–54
German church struggle, 96–103
German National Socialism, 97–98
Gilbert, Elizabeth, 56, 90
Gilkey, Langdon, 76–77
Gnosticism, 4, 89, 90, 132
God
   names for, 51, 109
   Scripture in seeking, 54
   as The Separation Maker, 73
   as a supreme being, 35–37
   worldview of, 37
good, evil and, 55–57, 89
grace alone, 6n13, 61

Haeckel, Ernst, 122

Hammurabi's moral code, 6
Hart, David Bentley, 30
Hawking, Stephen, 79, 128
Hebraism, 47
Hebrew Pentateuch, 45
Heidegger, Martin, 21, 29, 84
Hendry, George, 94
Hilary, 73
Hirsch, Emanuel, 103
Hitler, Adolf, 92, 98
holiness, in Leviticus, 108
Holy Trinity, 4, 24, 36, 81
Hübner, Kurt, 119–20
human life, mystery of, 34
humans
   dominion of, 71
   as image of God, 55

The If's and Ought's of Ethics (de Boer), 131
image of God, humans as, 55
immanence, 60
Institute on Religion and Public Life, 15, 20
Institutes of the Christian Religion (Calvin), 5, 20–21, 33, 104–5
integralism, 14, 21
"I-Thou" theology, 21, 29
Iwand, Hans, 97

Jaeger, Werner, 8
Jefferson, Thomas, 11
Jewish problem, final solution of, 97
Jobs, Steve, 90

Kant, Immanuel, 12–14, 43, 48, 50, 92
Kass, Leon, 109, 110–11
Kelly, J.N.D., 36
knowledge, limits of, 35–38
Kuyper, Abraham, 67–68, 73, 76, 105, 108–9

Lever, Jon, 113, 122
Lewis, C. S., 44
liberation theology, 29
liberation-read Marxist-theology, 14
life is religion, 14–22

Index

liminal thinking," 108
The Literal Meaning of Genesis (Augustine), 109
Locke, John, 11
Lucretius, 115–16
Luther, Martin, 65–66, 74
Lutheran church, 103

macro-evolutionism, 114–15, 120–31
Manicheanism, 89, 90
Marcion of Sinope, 4n6
Marcionism, 4
Marxist-theology, 14, 29
material world, 8
mathematical term "equality," 11
matter, continuous stream of, 127–28
meaning, fallacy of using, 13
Melchizedek, 6
Metamorphosis (Ovid poem), 128
meta-physical evolutionism, 133
metaphysical fallacy, 13
Midgley, Mary, 87, 106
Milton, John, 55, 89
modeling, 40–41
modern theory of evolutionism, 127
Moltmann, Jürgen, 95
monera, description of, 122
Moralistic Therapeutic Deism, 1
Morris, Henry, 26, 27
Moses
    projection of, 45–52
    use of week as sevenfold, 74–75
mystery, 33–35
myth, term usage, 47
Myths and Legends of Ancient Israel (Rappoport), 54–55

National Socialist ideology, 96–97, 102
natural reason, 56
natural sciences, 11, 115, 118–20
natural selection, 123
"nature and grace" motif, 8
Nazi society/state, 97–98, 101–2
Neo-Darwinians, 123–24
Neuhaus, Richard John, 15
New Modernism, 29
The New Modernism (Van Til), 17

Newton, Issac, 11
Nicholas of Cusa, 33
Nietzsche, Friedrich, 14
noetic cosmos, 7, 90
Nygren, Anders, 96

objectivity, scientific, 12
objectivity of reason, 12
On the Origin of the Species (Darwin), 121, 123, 130
ongoing creation, 58
Oparin, A. I., 122
Order Out of Chaos (Prigogine), 129
Origen, 8, 73
Otto, Rudolph, 33
"out of nothing" creation, 58–63, 92
Ovid (*Metamorphosis*), 128

paradise, 89
paradise lost, 89–91, 95
Paradise Lost (Milton), 55, 89
Pasteur, Louis, 121–22
perichoresis, 24
Peter, as first pope, 9
Philo of Alexandria, 8
Physiocrats, 11
Piersma, John Henry, 17
Plato, 7–8, 56, 90, 132
preservation, creation as and, 63–65
The Preservation of Favored Races in the Struggle for Life (Darwin), 121, 123, 130
Prigogine, Ilya, 117, 129–30
projection, 44, 47
Protestant Reformation, 10
Protestantism, Radical Orthodoxy, 14

Radical Orthodoxy, 14
Rappoport, Angelo, 54
real world, revelational content of Scripture, 25–28
reason
    first enlightenment and, 11
    objectivity of, 12
    science and, 11
Reformation, Protestant, 10, 24, 116
Reformed Church, Netherlands, 101

Index

religion
  the Church and, 9–10
  contemporary responses, 14–22
  distinguish false from true, 88
  dualism, 7–8
  first enlightenment, 11–12
  life is, 14–22
  marginalization, 7
  second enlightenment, 12–14
  silent diminishment, 7
restoration
  of creation, 56
  from sin, 88
revelation, two-foldness of Christian philosophy, 24–25, 31
Roman Catholic Church
  on Galileo, 40
  grace alone, 61
  as integralism, 14, 21
  natural law/natural theology, 91
  nature and grace model, 30
  Reformation and, 9
Rosenblatt, Naomi Harris, 90
Runner, H. Evan, 17

salvation
  Christian faith and, 2
  by grace alone, 6
  restoration of creation, 56
Schleiermacher, Friedrich, 58
scientific objectivity, 12
scientific speculation, 53–54
Scripture
  approach to, 38–44
  as its own interpreter, 23–24
  real world as revelational content of, 25–28
  in seeking God, 54
  Word spoken to listening humans, 25
second enlightenment, 12–14
secular eclipse of creation, 104–32, 133
secular theology, 17–22
separation, creation as
  division/separation differentiation, 65–72, 108–9
  out of nothing, 58–63
  preservation and, 63–65

separation blind, 111–18
separation of church from state, 9, 10
Simpson, G. G., 124–25
sin
  as perversion, 88
  willful transgression, 89
Smith, Christian, 1
spiritual, 8
spontaneous generation, 121–22
Spykman, Gordon, 110
Strauss, Leo, 68
The Structure of Scientific Theories (Suppe), 120
supernatural, 8, 11
Suppe, Frederick, 120

Tao, Torah and together, 28
taxonomy, evidence from, 126
Taylor, Barbara Brown, 37
theistic evolutionism, 104
theistic evolutionists, 14, 80–81, 114
theological theology, 21
theology
  necessity of Christian philosophy, 30–32
  in need of Christian philosophy, 28–29
theology, discipline of, 9–10
The Theology of Nature (Hendry), 94
Thirty Years War, 10
Thomas Aquinas, 5, 67n12
Tilgner, Wolfgang, 100
time
  creation and, 105–11
  defining of, 74, 75–76
  evolutionism and, 84
  myth of healing all wounds, 79
toledoth (Hebrew Pentateuch), 45–47, 89
transcendence, 60
Treaty of Westphalia, 10
Trinitarian theology, 4, 24, 36, 81
trinitarianism, 35
Trinity, 4, 24, 36, 81
Tyson, Paul, 19, 31n3, 39

understanding, Kant on, 12

Index

unity in Christ, 78
universal objectivity, 114

vain speculation, 52
Van Leeuwen, Raymond, 108
Van Til, Cornelius, 17
Vander Goot, early years, 15–17
the "very good" of creation, 55–57
viruses, discovery of, 123
Voegelin, Eric, 4n6
Volksnomostheologies und Schöpfungsglaube (Tilgner), 100
von Rad, Gerhard, 93

Wars of Religion, 10, 11, 18, 19, 114
waste and void, first creation, 60
Webster, John, 21

week, as sevenfold design, 74
Wellhausen, Julius, 51
Westermann, Claus, 93–94
White, Lynn, 71–72
"whose region, his religion," 10
Wingren, Gustaf, 2, 91, 96–97, 103
Wolf, Ernst, 97
"works righteousness," 19

Young, Norman, 93
Younger Testament
    term usage, 2, 2n4
    two-foldness of, 24

Zaslow, David, 2
Zoroastrianism, 89

www.ingramcontent.com/pod-product-compliance
Lightning Source LLC
Chambersburg PA
CBHW071211160426
43196CB00011B/2261